Short Cuts

Dedication

To my wife, the finest teacher I know, who tested chapters in her classroom, gave suggestions, even helped proofread despite her busy schedule—but most of all, gave me encouragement when it was most needed.

James Mentel
Los Angeles Unified School District

The McGraw-Hill Companies, Inc.
New York St. Louis San Francisco Auckland
Bogotá Caracas Lisbon London Madrid Mexico City
Milan Montreal New Delhi San Juan Singapore
Sydney Tokyo Toronto

McGraw-Hill 
A Division of The ***McGraw-Hill*** *Companies*

Short Cuts
An Interactive English Course
Book One

1 2 3 4 5 6 7 8 9 0 VNH VNH 9 0 9 8 7 6

ISBN 0-07-041886-1
ISBN 0-07-114518-4

This book was set in Caslon Regular by York Graphic Services, Inc. The editors were Tim Stookesberry and Kathy Melee; the art editor was Delight Avôké; the interior designer was Niza Hanany, the front and back matter designer was Suzanne Montazer; the production supervisors were Tanya Nigh and Michelle Lyon; the cover was designed by Francis Owens; the cover and interior illustrator was Dave Sullivan; interior icons were designed by Marcus Badgley; editorial and production assistance was provided by Pam Tiberia, Pam Webster, Jane Parkinson, and Deborah Bruce.

Von Hoffman Press, Jefferson City, MO, was printer and binder.
Phoenix Color Corporation was cover separator and printer.

Library of Congress Catalog Card Number: 95-82144

INTERNATIONAL EDITION

When ordering this title, use ISBN 0-07-114518-4

Contents

From the Author viii
To the Teacher ix
A Visual Tour x
About the Supplements xvi

STRUCTURE GOALS	COMPETENCIES	RECOGNITION

CHAPTER

1 School 1

Students will have a sense of the form of . . .
- **be** in the present tense
  - affirmative statements
  - contractions
- questions with **where**
- sentences with subject (+) **be** (+) prepositional phrase

Students will be *able to . . .*
- understand and use school vocabulary
- give and understand directions
- ask for the location of a person or place
- understand and use the numbers 1-100
- ask for clarification

Students may understand and use some examples of . . .
- pauses, hesitations, and false starts in listening

CHAPTER

2 A Kitchen 13

Students will have a sense of the form of . . .
- **be** in the present tense
  - questions
- singular and plural count nouns
- pronouns

Students will be able to . . .
- understand and use vocabulary related to cooking and eating
- make a polite request
- make an offer of help
- express simple needs
- express thanks

Students may understand and use some examples of . . .
- present continuous tense
- imperative form
- varieties of register (formal, less formal answers)

CHAPTER

3 Time 25

Students will have a sense of the form of . . .
- **be** in the present tense
  - negative statements
- questions about time
- intensifiers (*very late*)

Students will be able to . . .
- understand and use time vocabulary
- ask for and give the time
- describe location
- apologize for a situation

Students may understand and use some examples of . . .
- present continuous tense
- frequency adverbs
- simple present tense of additional verbs

STRUCTURE GOALS	COMPETENCIES	RECOGNITION

CHAPTER 8 **Your Body** 85

Students will have a sense of the form of . . . • simple present tense with **does** questions negative statements	*Students will be able to . . .* • understand and use health and body vocabuary • ask about and report common medical problems • introduce yourself • call in sick	*Students may understand and use some examples of . . .* • past tense of **be** • past tense of additional verbs

CHAPTER 9 **The Family** 97

Students will have a sense of the form of . . . • possessive adjectives • the possessive **'s**	*Students will be able to . . .* • understand and use family vocabulary • ask and answer questions about the family • introduce someone to another person	*Students may understand and use some examples of . . .* • present perfect tense • past tense of additional verbs

CHAPTER 10 **A Daily Schedule** 109

Students will have a sense of the form of . . . • frequency adverbs	*Students will be able to . . .* • understand and use vocabulary related to daily schedules • describe a typical schedule • ask for additional information when an answer is negative	*Students may understand and use some examples of . . .* • past tense of additional verbs

Verb Charts 121
Dialogues 129
Worksheets 139

From the Author

Dear Colleagues,

I developed these materials by trying out ideas in real adult English classrooms over many years. I was influenced by theories and research about language acquisition, but in the end, what influenced me most was what worked. The things that worked are here in the book—the things that didn't work, are not. Most of all, my goal was to provide teachers with tools that would allow their natural creativity to bloom. I've been continually amazed at the creativity of ESOL teachers, and all too often materials have confined that creativity rather than encouraged it.

These are materials, not a method. My hope is that they are like a very solid, well-made tool that a carpenter can use day after day in many different ways and situations, creating many different projects. Although the **Teacher's Manual** provides exact, step-by-step directions about one way to use the materials, I've been happy to find that almost all teachers who have used the materials have come up with their own creative ways to use them, ways that fit their own teaching style and student population.

As teachers, we are all explorers and researchers. The more we explore and invent, the more exciting language teaching becomes, and the more exciting language learning becomes. I hope you will share some of your results with me by writing me in care of my publisher.

I feel extremely fortunate to be publishing these materials with McGraw-Hill, and I'd like to thank a number of people there for their intelligence, bravery, and good humor throughout the entire process. I would especially like to thank my editors: Tim Stookesberry, who "got it" right from the beginning, and Cheryl Pavlik, for never letting me get away with anything. I would also like to acknowledge the rest of the editorial and production team who worked so painstakingly on these materials: Kathy Melee, Tanya Nigh, Francis Owens, Delight Avoke, Michelle Lyon, Catherine Sessions, Bill Preston, Gina Martinez, Pam Tiberia, and the wonderfully talented artist, Dave Sullivan. Finally, I'd like to thank Thalia Dorwick, Carole O'Keefe, Tom Allumbaugh, Roxan Kinsey, Margaret Metz, and the rest of the McGraw-Hill sales and marketing department for their outstanding support.

Sincerely,

To the Teacher

Short Cuts is a three-level series for teaching English to young adult and adult students. Each level of the program contains the following components:

1. a student text
2. a teacher's manipulative kit (available in two versions)
3. an optional teacher's audio tape
4. an optional student audio tape
5. a teacher's manual

Using Manipulatives

A unique feature of ***Short Cuts*** is its use of manipulatives, or cut-ups. The use of these manipulatives:

- addresses a variety of learning styles: visual, aural, and kinesthetic;
- provides immediate feedback for both teacher and student;
- focuses students' attention on accomplishing specific tasks during an extended receptive period;
- encourages the use of English for the negotiation of meaning through student interaction;
- provides opportunities for student-centered cooperative learning.

Perhaps the best reasons for using manipulatives are that they are fun, they create student interest and they work! Using them is a little like playing a computer game, and it's a lot more fun to do that than to sit passively and listen to the teacher. The manipulatives in the ***Short Cuts*** program have been used with grandmothers and gang-members, and the reaction has always been positive.

The teacher is also provided with his/her own manipulatives that can be used to model language and for other communicative classroom activities. The teacher's version of both the worksheet and manipulatives is found in the ***Teacher's Manipulative Kit*** (see description on page xvi).

Each of the ten chapters in the student text is organized around a theme. The accompanying student worksheets and manipulatives used to complete many of the exercises and activities in the chapters correspond to these themes. The student worksheets and manipulatives are located in perforated pages at the back of the student text. The smaller pictures along the side and bottom of the worksheets are the manipulatives—they should be cut or torn out. The ***Teacher's Manual*** contains many more helpful suggestions for ways to use these materials in the classroom.

Recommended Proficiency Levels

Book One of the ***Short Cuts*** program is designed for low-beginning students. Typically, students at this level have little or no ability to read and write in English. They may know a few isolated words or phrases, but they have difficulty understanding even the simplest conversations. They may only be able to communicate with native speakers through gestures or a few very halting words. This level has been written to correspond directly to the ESL Beginning-Low level in the California Model Standards.

Short Cuts is compatible with the Comprehensive Adult Student Assessment System (CASAS) and the Student Performance Levels (SPLs) recommended by the Mainstream English Language Training (MELT) project of the U.S. Department of Health and Human Services. SPL scores shown below are correlated with scores on the Basic English Skills Test (BEST).

Grammar coverage can also be used to determine placement. ***Short Cuts, Book One*** contains the following grammar topics: simple present, simple past (for recognition only), present continuous.

	MELT SPLs	BEST Scores	CASAS Achievements Scores
Short Cuts Book One	O and I	0–15	165–190
Short Cuts Book Two	II	16–28	181–190
Short Cuts Book Three	III	29–41	191–208

A Visual Tour of This Text

This visual tour is designed to acquaint you with the key features of the student textbook, as well as to give you suggestions of at least one way to teach those features.

The essential teaching elements for the ***Short Cuts*** program are self-contained in the student text. This book provides between 100–130 hours of instruction in all four language skills—listening, speaking, reading, and writing—as well as additional instruction in the essential grammar structures typically introduced at this level.

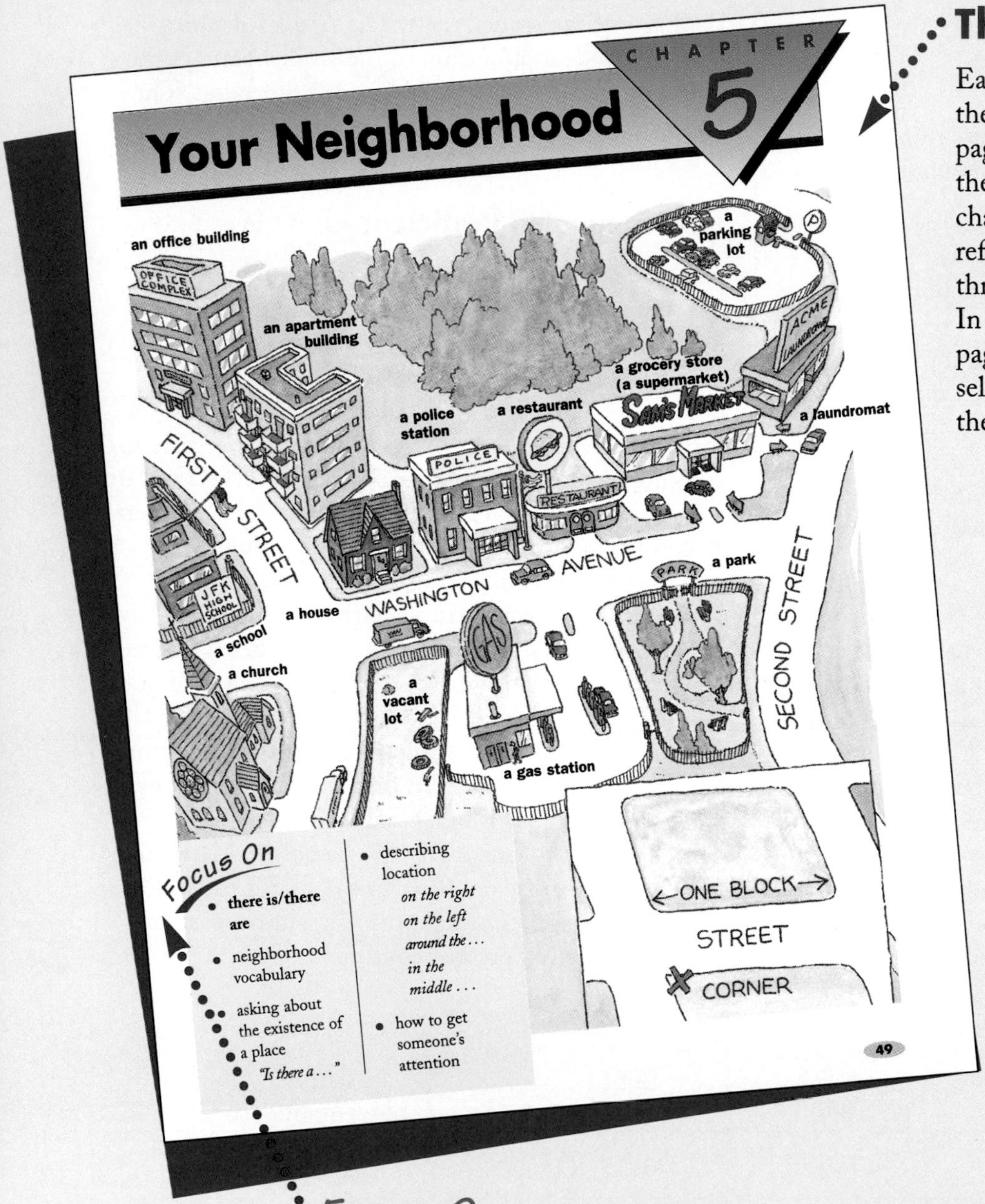

The Opening Page

Each chapter revolves around a central theme or content focus. The opening page is a visual depiction of this theme and includes most of the key chapter vocabulary. It also serves as a reference for students as they work through each section of the chapter. In addition, students refer back to this page to check their answers in the self-review **On Your Own** section at the end of the chapter.

Focus On

The **Focus On** box gives both teachers and students a quick glance at the most important elements of the chapter.

The Worksheet

Located in perforated pages in the back of the student text, the worksheet contains a simplified version of the picture found in the chapter opener, as well as the student manipulatives. This page should be torn out every time the class is ready to start a new chapter in ***Short Cuts***, as it will be the focus for many of the activities in each lesson.

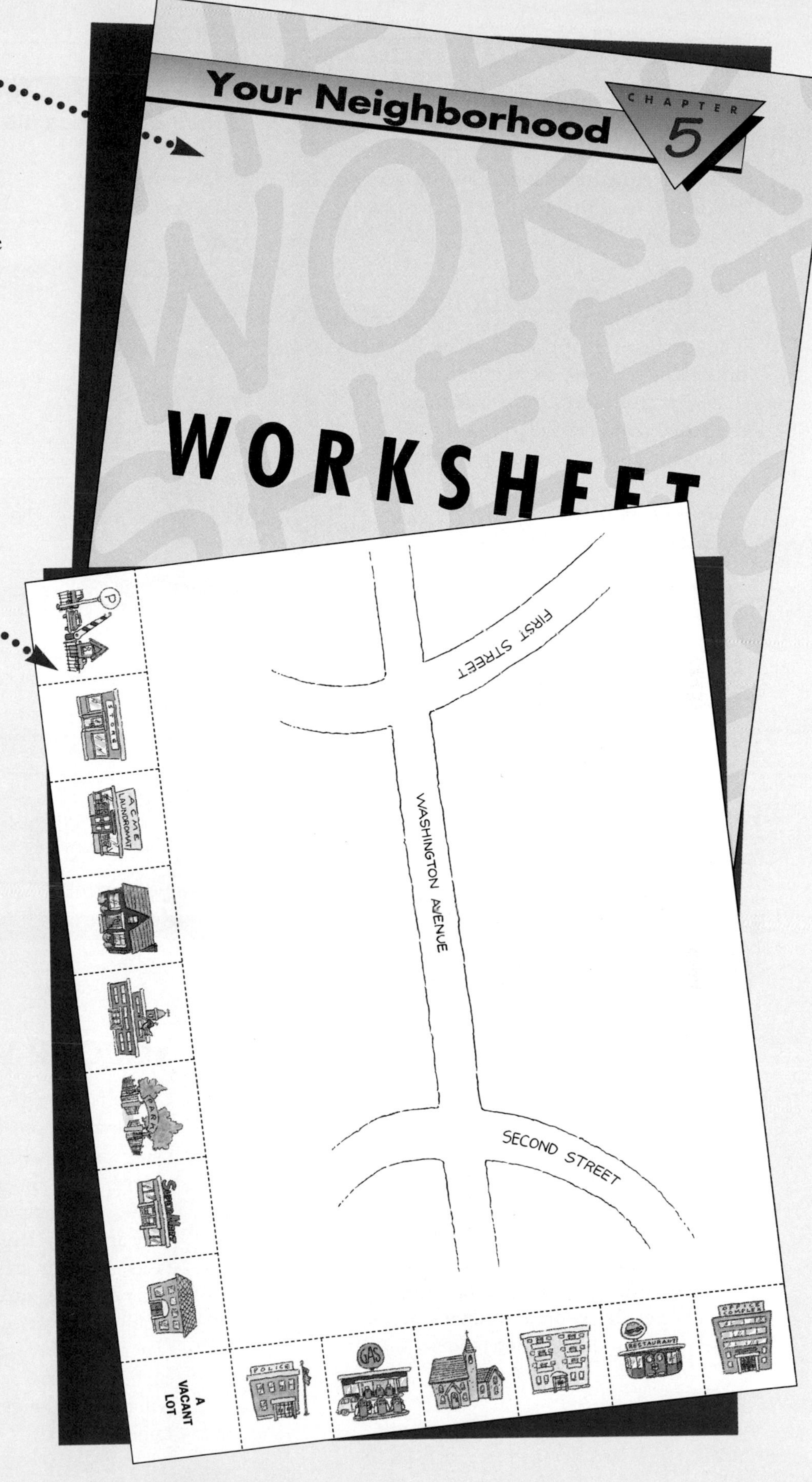

Manipulatives

The manipulatives, or cut-outs, are the pictures found at the edges of the worksheet. Students will either tear or cut them out with scissors and move them around on their worksheets to complete many of the listening, speaking, reading, and writing activities found in the chapter.

Tips on Using the Worksheet

The ***Teacher's Manual*** includes a number of suggestions on how to use the worksheet and manipulatives. It's a good idea to encourage your students to collect and store their manipulatives with either a paperclip or an envelope at the end of each lesson. You should also keep a few extra photocopies of the worksheet page on hand for emergencies!

A TYPICAL CHAPTER LESSON

Each chapter contains four two-page sections (called **Situations**) which practice all four skills and are meant to be self-contained lessons lasting 2–3 hours.

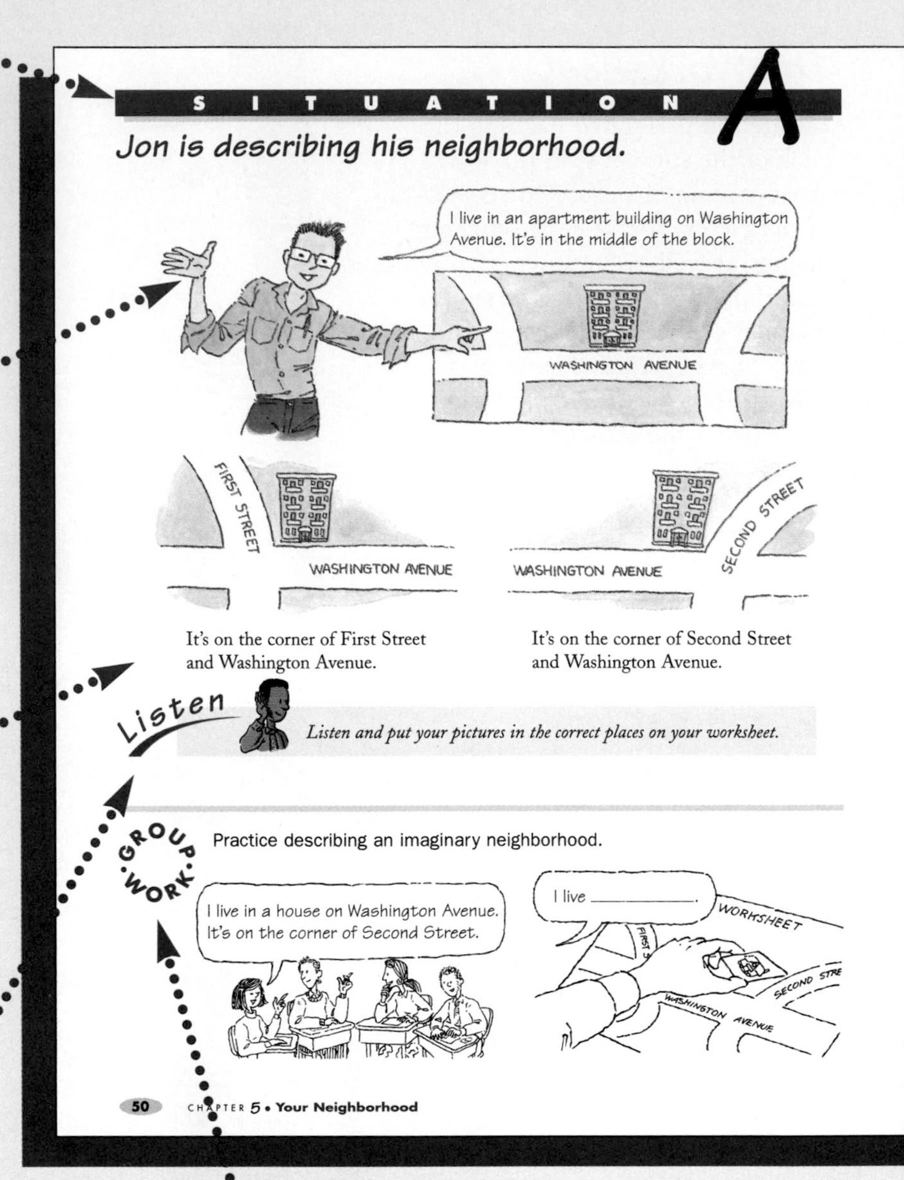

SITUATION A
Jon is describing his neighborhood.
I live in an apartment building on Washington Avenue. It's in the middle of the block.
WASHINGTON AVENUE
FIRST STREET
WASHINGTON AVENUE
WASHINGTON AVENUE
SECOND STREET
It's on the corner of First Street and Washington Avenue.
It's on the corner of Second Street and Washington Avenue.
Listen
Listen and put your pictures in the correct places on your worksheet.
GROUP WORK
Practice describing an imaginary neighborhood.
I live in a house on Washington Avenue. It's on the corner of Second Street.
I live ______.
WORKSHEET
SECOND STREET
WASHINGTON AVENUE
50 CHAPTER 5 • Your Neighborhood

A Visual Introduction

The teacher begins the lesson by presenting a chunk of language using materials from the ***Teacher's Kit*** and the visual dialogue found in the **Situation**. In this sample, the chunk includes *I live in a house, I live in an apartment, on (a street)* as well as *in the middle of the block* and *on the corner of (a street).*

Examples

The examples are visual references for any extra information students may need to do the listening and group work.

Listening Exercises

After the target language has been adequately modeled, students arrange their worksheet pictures in response to a listening activity conducted by the teacher. The teacher has many options here—she/he can use the ***Teacher's Tape*** that is provided for these sections or the tapescript in the back of the student text to conduct this period of active listening. This section gives students the opportunity to be actively involved in a fun and challenging activity without having to produce language. By looking at the students' worksheets, the teacher gets immediate feedback on how much each student understands.

•GROUP WORK•

Students form groups and practice on their own. In most instances, they will be using their worksheet in response to various tasks and activities associated with the lesson's main teaching focus. Since they are using language to do specific tasks, students are forced to listen carefully and negotiate meaning. Often this requires the use of clarification devices. (*I'm sorry. Was that left or right?*) Because such interactive activities are fun, students will practice longer and with more sustained interest.

Reading

Read this, and put your pictures in the correct places on your worksheet.

I live in a small house on Washington Avenue. It's on the corner of Second Street. Next to my house, on the left, there's a parking lot. Next to the parking lot, there's a gas station.

Clear your worksheet. Now read this.

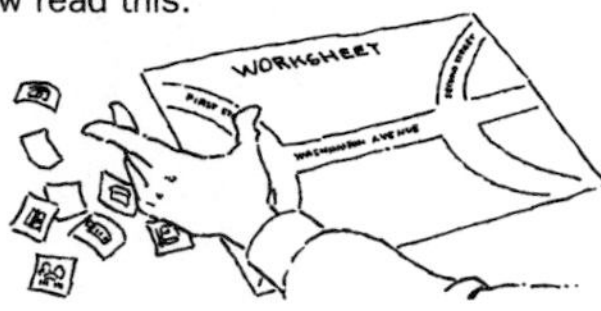

I live in an apartment building on Washington Avenue. It's in the middle of the block. Next to my apartment building, on the right, there's a police station. Next to the police station, there's a school.

Now clear your worksheet again.

Writing

Write about your street.

I live in ______________________________________
(a house / an apartment building)

on ______________________________________. On the right of my
(name of your street)

______________________ there is ______________________
(house / apartment building)

______________. Next to that is a ______________________.

Extra *Read your story to the class or your group. They will put their pictures in the correct places on their worksheets.*

Reading

There are two types of readings in this book. The first type, as shown in this example, is a strict reinforcement of the oral and listening material. Here, students can—on their own or with a partner or group—arrange their manipulatives on their worksheets to reflect the information found in the reading passage. Again, the teacher can immediately check comprehension by circulating around class during this activity. The second type of reading often found in ***Short Cuts*** uses either a simple labeling of vocabulary or a written task to give a purpose to understanding the reading passage.

Writing

The writing activity is usually independent of the reading. As in this example, the reading section often models a particular type of writing and then asks the student to complete the writing to reflect her/his own information, real or imagined. Often students can arrange their manipulatives on their worksheet as a kind of brainstorming activity. Then, by circulating throughout the classroom, the teacher will be able to see what the student is trying to write about and be able to offer the kind of help that's needed. Most of the writing activities in ***Short Cuts*** offer enough flexibility to allow students a lot of room for personal communication in their writing—there are rarely "right or wrong" answers.

Extra

Sprinkled throughout all chapters, the **Extra** boxes provide students with an additional twist on a given chapter activity. In this example, students are encouraged to read their writing passages aloud to their group or the whole class, who will then use the information to complete a listening activity.

GRAMMAR CHECK

This two-page spread is meant to introduce the important structural element(s) of the chapter. On the left-hand page, there is a visual introduction to the topic at hand, in this instance, *there is/there are*. Pictures from the chapter are used to contextualize the grammar topic in a very simple fashion. Note: although the **Grammar Check** section appears at the end of each chapter, teachers may introduce it at any point in the lesson (at their own discretion).

GRAMMAR CHECK

There is / there are

When we describe places we often use **there is** or **there are:**

There **is** a church in **my neighborhood.**

When we speak, we usually make a contraction:

There's a church in **my neighborhood.**

Two or more things use **are:**

There **are** two churches in **my neighborhood.**

Here's how we use **not** to make negative statements.

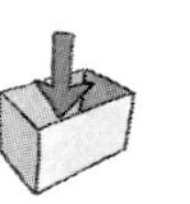

a church in **my neighborhood.**

any churches in **my neighborhood.**

THERE IS / THERE ARE

AFFIRMATIVE STATEMENTS

There is There's	a church a parking lot a park	on the right corner. on the left corner. around the corner. next to my house.
There are	two churches three houses	

NEGATIVE STATEMENTS

There isn't There's not	a church a parking lot a park	in this neighborhood. around here.
There aren't	any churches any houses any parks	

YES / NO QUESTIONS AND ANSWERS

Is there	a church a parking lot	around here	?
Are there	any stores any gas stations		

Yes, there is.	No, there isn't.
Yes, there are.	No, there aren't.

•EXERCISE•

Look at the picture on page 49. Fill in the blanks in this story about the picture. Use **there is, there are**, or **there aren't** (any).

1. There is ______ a house next to the police station.
2. ______ ten cars in the parking lot.
3. ______ four trees in the park.
4. ______ an apartment building around the corner from the house.
5. ______ any cars in the vacant lot.
6. ______ a grocery store across from the park.
7. ______ any people in the vacant lot.
8. ______ a high school on the corner of First Street and Washington Avenue.
9. ______ two cars at the grocery store.
10. ______ a laundromat next to the grocery store, on the right.

GRAMMAR CHECK 59

GRAMMAR BOXES

The right-hand page includes more traditional grammar boxes that students can use as a reference to complete the exercise that follows.

•EXERCISES•

The grammar exercises are completely tied to the context of the chapter's theme. They usually refer in some way to the picture on the opening page.

ON YOUR OWN

This page is designed to be used as a chapter review after the students have completed all of the chapter's lessons.

ON YOUR OWN

Vocabulary

Do you know these words? Find them on page 49.

- ❑ an office building
- ❑ an apartment building
- ❑ a school
- ❑ a house
- ❑ a police station
- ❑ a restaurant
- ❑ a grocery store
- ❑ a laundromat
- ❑ a parking lot
- ❑ a vacant lot
- ❑ a church
- ❑ a gas station
- ❑ a park
- ❑ one block
- ❑ street
- ❑ corner

Listening

Listen to your tape, and put your pictures in the correct places on your worksheet. Then check your answer on page 49.

Becky: My neighborhood is nice. I live in a small house. It's on the corner of Washington and First. Next to my house, on the right, there's a police station. There's a restaurant next to the police station. Around the corner from my house, there's an apartment building. It's a big apartment building.

Across from my house, there's a vacant lot, right on the corner. Next to the vacant lot, there's a big gas station. On the corner of Second Street, next to the gas station, there's a park. On the other corner of my block, across from the park, there's a grocery store. Around the corner from the store, there's a laundromat.

How to
get the attention of a stranger
Excuse me, sir.
Yes?
Excuse me, ma'am.
Yes?
60
CHAPTER 5 • Your Neighborhood

Vocabulary

These are the key vocabulary items that students are expected to master by the end of the chapter. All of these words also appear on the ***Student Audio Cassette*** for additional help in pronunciation.

Listening

Appearing on the ***Student Audio Cassette***, this dialogue acts as a final test for comprehension for the student. The most important elements studied in the chapter appear in this listening passage in an authentic slice of dialogue, with expanded vocabulary. The student listens to the tape (or to the teacher), places his or her manipulatives on the worksheet, and then checks his or her answers against the picture found on the opening page of the chapter.

How to

These boxes are visual representations of useful language functions.

About the Supplements

All the supplemental materials included in the ***Short Cuts*** program work together to help you provide a truly communicative learning experience for your students. We've purposefully tried to design classroom materials that are flexible so you can adapt them to your individual needs. We encourage you to mix and match these supplements to fit your particular teaching style and classroom configuration.

Teacher's Manipulative Kit—Poster Version

This kit contains:

Ten posters
Plastic student manipulatives

The ***Teacher's Manipulative Kit*** is available in two different versions. The first version is a series of 10 posters that directly corresponds to the student worksheets found in the text. These oversized posters are printed on a specially treated paper so that the plastic manipulatives will stick on them, in much the same fashion as refrigerator magnets! The posters are large enough so students in the back of the room will be able to see them clearly.

When you order the posters to accompany this text, they come packaged with a complete set of plastic manipulatives that you can use to model all of the exercises in the text. Again, these manipulatives directly mirror those found on the student worksheets in the text. There is also an extra blank sheet of plastic included in the poster kit so you can make your own manipulatives for additional vocabulary items and classroom activities.

Optional Teacher's Easel

A portable ***Teacher's Easel*** is available for use with the ***Teacher's Poster Kit***. Made of durable cardboard stock, this lightweight instructor's resource comes in a box that is also suitable for storing the complete supplemental package (posters, manipulatives, audio tapes, etc.).

Teacher's Manipulative Kit—Transparency Version

This kit contains:

Ten transparency acetates

Another option, for those teachers with access to an overhead projector, is the version of the ***Teacher's Manipulative Kit*** in transparency acetate form. These acetates directly model those found in the student text and come in a special binder equipped to store the manipulatives after you're done using them in class. This version of the kit can also be used in conjunction with the poster version to create information gaps, or to model two different situations simultaneously.

Optional Teacher's Audio-Cassette Tape

This audio-cassette tape contains all of the dialogues found in the **Listen** sections of each lesson of the book. There are four separate **Listen** sections in each chapter, one on each of the four separate **Situation** pages.

Because it might not always be convenient for you to carry a tape player to class, we've provided the tapescripts for these sections in the back of the student text, again on perforated pages. You can simply read the tapescript aloud yourself to model the dialogues, or you can assign different roles to your students to make this section an even more interactive exercise.

Optional Student's Audio-Cassette Tape

Although you might choose to use the student audio-cassette tape in class or in a language laboratory setting, it was designed to be used as a self-study aid for students working on their own. All of the materials found on this tape are listed on the last page of each chapter in the **On Your Own** section.

Teacher's Manual

Written by the author, the ***Teacher's Manual*** to accompany this text is full of helpful ideas and suggestions for using all of the materials in the ***Short Cuts*** program. Although these materials can be adapted to virtually any teaching method or style, the ***Teacher's Manual*** gives detailed suggestions about a variety of class-tested ways that the materials have worked for the author and his colleagues. It also contains detailed lesson plans for each chapter of the book, optional exercises and activities, recommended ways of dealing with authentic materials in the classroom, and much more.

CHAPTER 1

School

Focus On

- **be** in present tense
- affirmative statements
- school vocabulary
- numbers 1–100
- giving directions
  next to
  across from
  in
- how to ask for clarification

SITUATION 

Antonio is registering for a class.

Room 2 is **across from** the cafeteria.

Room 2 is **next to** the cafeteria.

1 one	3 three	5 five	7 seven	9 nine
2 two	4 four	6 six	8 eight	10 ten

Listen

Listen and put your pictures in the correct places on your worksheet.

GROUP WORK

STEP 1

Form a group.

STEP 2

Tell your classmates your name.

STEP 3

Make a map of a school.

STEP 4

Put your pictures on your worksheet.

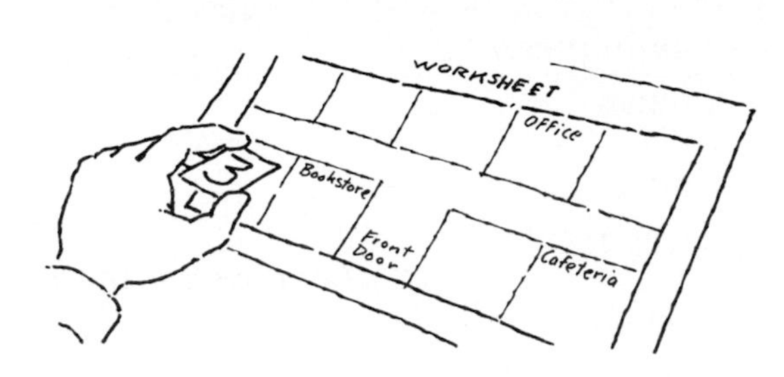

Reading

Read this, and put your pictures in the correct places.

1. Room 2 is next to the bookstore.
2. Room 4 is across from the office.
3. The men's room is across from the cafeteria.
4. Room 6 is across from the bookstore.
5. The women's room is next to the office.
6. Room 3 is across from room 2.

Now clear your worksheet to make another map.

Writing

Step One Put room numbers on your worksheet.

Step Two Write six sentences about your worksheet. There are no right or wrong answers.

1. ______________________________
2. ______________________________
3. ______________________________
4. ______________________________
5. ______________________________
6. ______________________________

Read your sentences to the group or to the class. Your classmates will put their pictures in the correct places on their worksheets.

SITUATION 

Carmen is asking for directions.

11 eleven	18 eighteen	25 twenty-five	50 fifty
12 twelve	19 nineteen	26 twenty-six	60 sixty
13 thirteen	20 twenty	27 twenty-seven	70 seventy
14 fourteen	21 twenty-one	28 twenty-eight	80 eighty
15 fifteen	22 twenty-two	29 twenty-nine	90 ninety
16 sixteen	23 twenty-three	30 thirty	100 one-hundred
17 seventeen	24 twenty-four	40 forty	

Listen and put your pictures in the correct places on your worksheet.

Make a group, and practice questions like these. Use your worksheet.

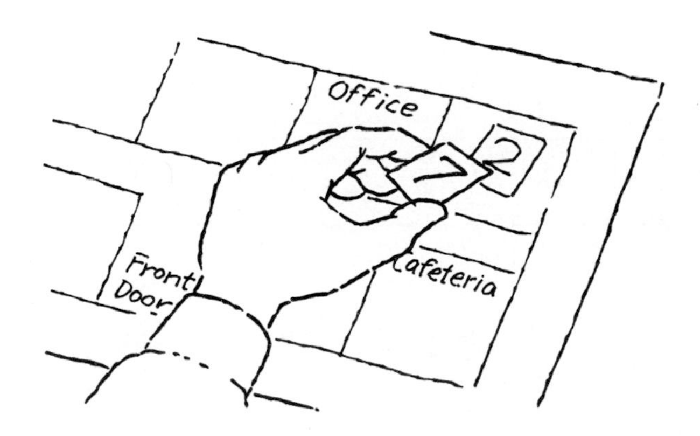

Reading/Writing

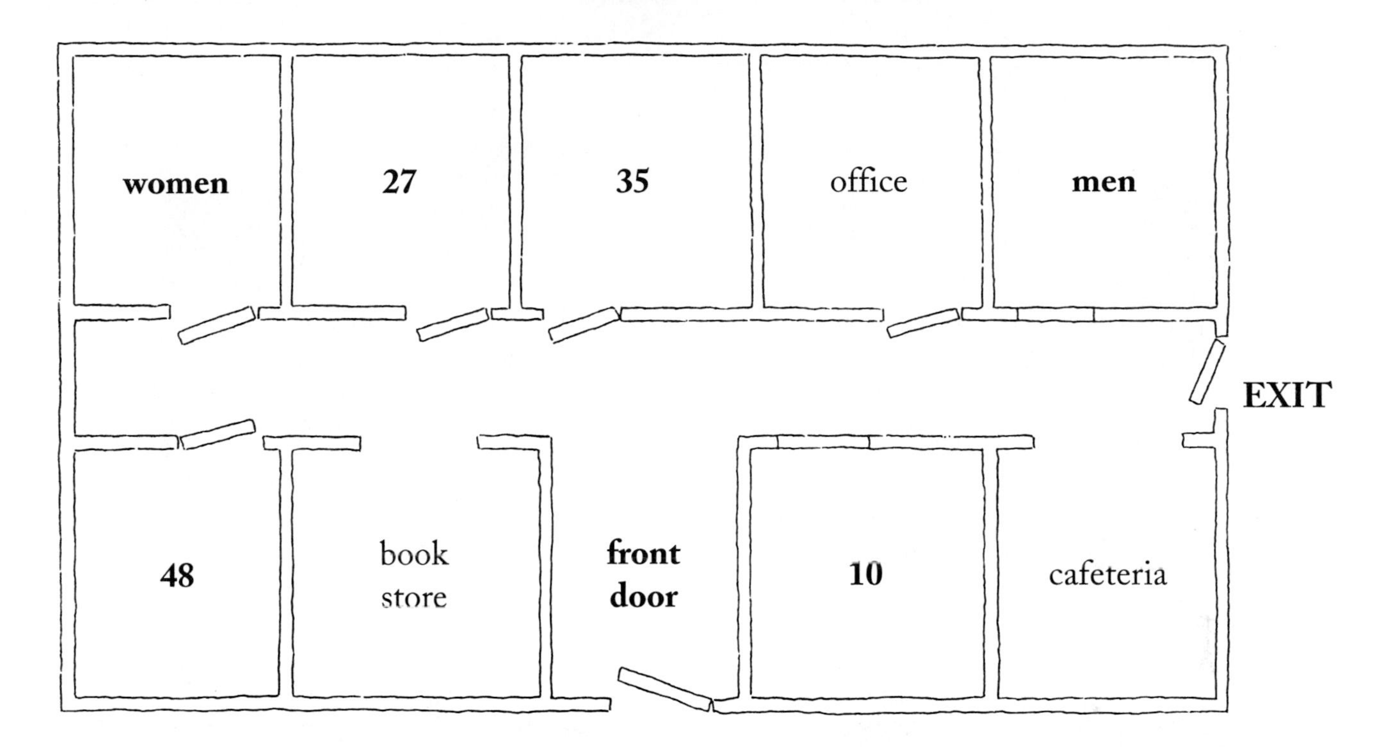

My School

This is a map of my school. I study English here. The office is near the front door. My class is in room 27. Room 27 is across (1) from (2) the bookstore. Room 48 is ________ (3) ________ (4) the bookstore. My friend is in room 10. Room 10 is ________ (5) ________ (6) the cafeteria. The women's room is ________ (7) ________ (8) room 27. The men's room is ________ (9) ________ (10) the cafeteria.

Extra *Work in groups. Make a map of your school.*

SITUATION

C

Magda is looking for her teacher.

Excuse me. Where's Mr. Sanchez?
He's in room 7.
Where's room 7?
Across from the bookstore.
7
Where's Mr. Sanchez?
He's in room 7.
8
Where's Ms. Williams?
She's in room 8.

Listen

Listen and put your pictures in the correct places on your worksheet.

GROUP WORK

Make a group. Ask and answer questions like these. Use your worksheet.

Where's Ms. Williams?
She's in room 8.

Where's that?
It's ____ ____.

Reading

Read this, and put your pictures in the correct place on your worksheet.

1. Ms. Williams teaches English 1. She's in room 21. It's next to the bookstore.
2. Mr. Sanchez teaches English 2. He's in room 46. It's across from the office.
3. The men's room is across from the cafeteria. The women's room is across from room 21.
4. Room 37 is next to the women's room. Nobody is in the room right now. It's empty.
5. Room 50 is between room 37 and the office.

Now close your books. Look at your picture. What can you remember?

Writing

Write about yourself and your school. Complete the information.

1. My name is ______________________________.
   name
2. My teacher is ______________________________.
   name
3. My room number is ______________________________.
4. The school secretary is ______________________________.
   name
5. The school janitor is ______________________________.
   name
6. The librarian is ______________________________.
   name
7. Three of my classmates are ______________________________,
   name
   ____________________, and ____________________.
   name *name*

SITUATION

May is giving directions.

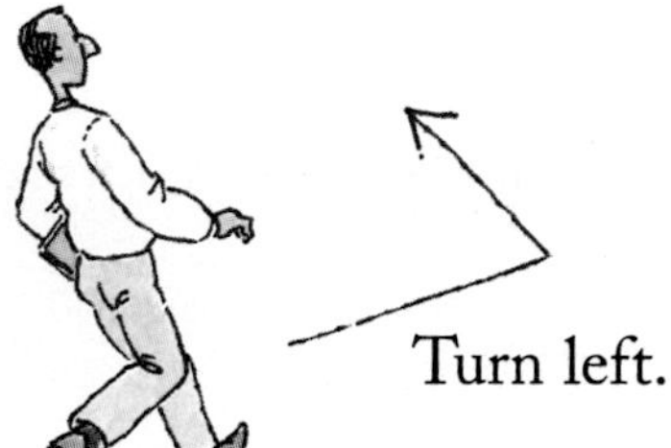

Listen

Look at the map. You are at the front door. Listen and follow the directions.

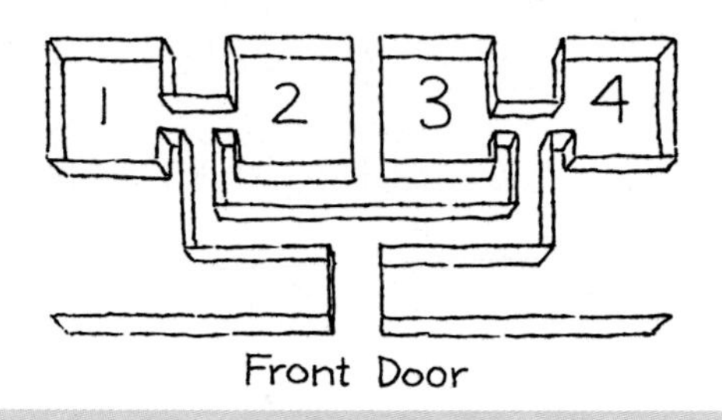

GROUP WORK

Make a group. Use the map above. You are at the front door. Give directions to room 1, 2, 3, or 4.

Reading

Read this, and do the puzzle.

1. Go straight.
2. Turn left.
3. Go straight.
4. Turn right.
5. Turn right again.
6. Go straight and turn left.
7. Then turn left again.
8. Now turn right.
9. Turn right again.

Where are you?

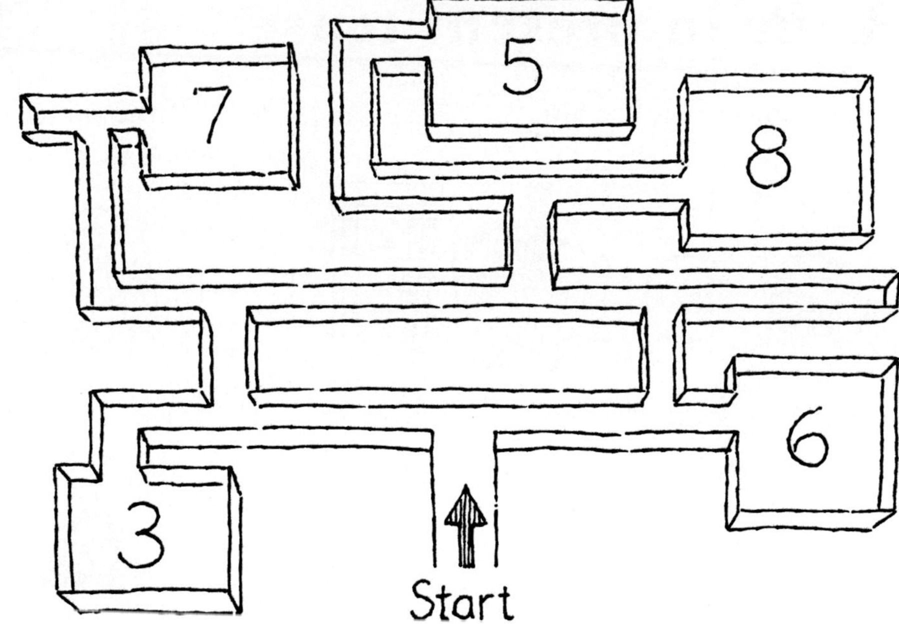

Writing

Write directions to one of the rooms in the puzzle.

A. *Be* in present tense

If the subject is I, use **am.**

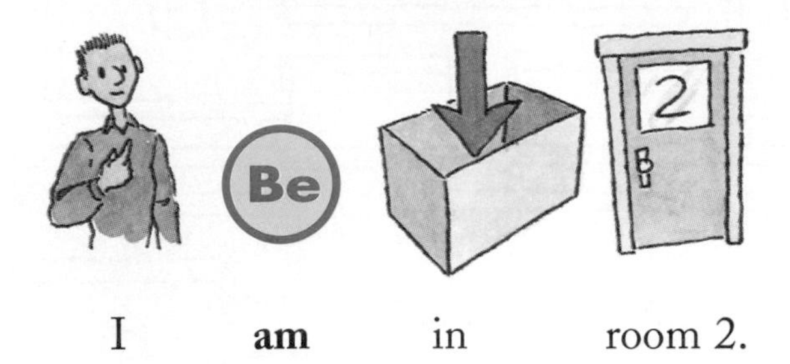

I **am** in room 2.

If the subject is one man, one woman or one thing, use **is.**

Mr. Sanchez **is** in room 2.

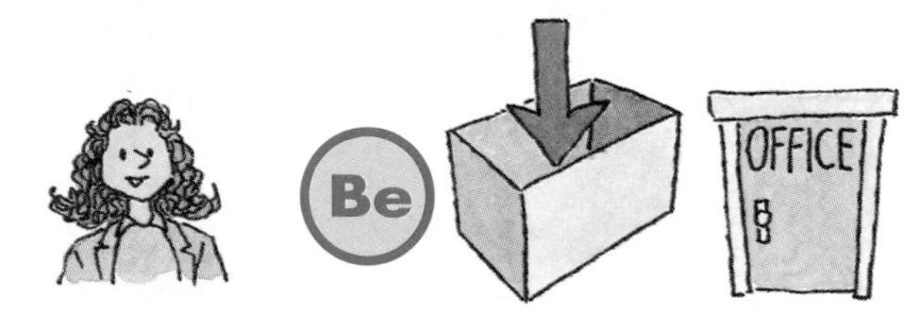

Ms. Williams **is** in the office.

Room 3 **is** next to room 4.

B. Contractions

When we speak, we usually say the subject and **be** together. We call this a *contraction* and we write it like this:

I **am** ⟶ I'm

He **is** ⟶ He's

She **is** ⟶ She's

It **is** ⟶ It's

LOCATION QUESTIONS AND ANSWERS WITH **BE**

QUESTION WORD	BE	SUBJECT	
Where	am	I	?
	is 's	Mr. Sanchez he room 3 it Ms. Williams she	
	are	you they	

SUBJECT	BE		
I	am 'm	in next to across from	room 3. room 2. the office. the bookstore.
She Ms. Williams He Mr. Sanchez Room 3 It	is 's		
We You They	are 're		

•EXERCISE•

Look at page 1. Complete the answers to the questions. Write **He's, She's** or **It's.**

1. Where's the office? ___It's___ next to room 24.
2. Where's Mr. Sanchez? __________ in room 7.
3. Where's the secretary? __________ in the office.
4. Where's the men's room? __________ next to the bookstore.
5. Where's room 13? __________ across from the office.
6. Where's the janitor? __________ in the hall.
7. Where's the cafeteria? __________ next to room 13.
8. Where's the clerk? __________ in the bookstore.

Write more sentences about the picture on page 1.

ON YOUR OWN

Vocabulary

Do you know these words? Find them on page 1.

- ❑ school
- ❑ secretary
- ❑ office
- ❑ student
- ❑ teacher
- ❑ classroom
- ❑ women's room
- ❑ janitor
- ❑ hall
- ❑ exit
- ❑ cafeteria
- ❑ blackboard
- ❑ desk
- ❑ chair
- ❑ bookstore
- ❑ clerk
- ❑ men's room
- ❑ front door

Listening

Listen to your tape and put your pictures in the correct places on your worksheet. Then check your answer on page 1.

Carmen: Excuse me. Where's room thirteen?
Mr. Young: It's across from the office.
Carmen: Thanks.

May: Excuse me.
Jack: Yes?
May: Where's room eight?
Jack: Eight?
May: Yes.
Jack: It's across from the bookstore.
May: Thanks a lot.

Magda: Excuse me. Where's the women's room?
Mrs. Bixby: It's next to *(cough)*.
Magda: Excuse me?
Mrs. Bixby: Next to room eight.
Magda: Oh. Thanks.

Becky: Excuse me, where's room twenty-four?
Bookstore clerk: Twenty-four? Let's see . . . uh . . . I think it's across from the cafeteria. Next to the office over there.
Becky: Thank you.

How to
ask for clarification

Excuse me. Where's room 3?
It's next to the cafeteria.
I'm sorry. Could you repeat that?
Sure. It's next to the cafeteria.

CHAPTER 2

A Kitchen

Focus On

- **be** in present tense
  - singular/plural nouns
- pronouns
- kitchen and food vocabulary
- cooking verbs
- **in** and **on**
- polite requests
  - *"Could you put . . . ?"*
- how to thank someone

S I T U A T I O N

Minh is visiting Maria. They're putting away groceries.

Could you put the tomatoes

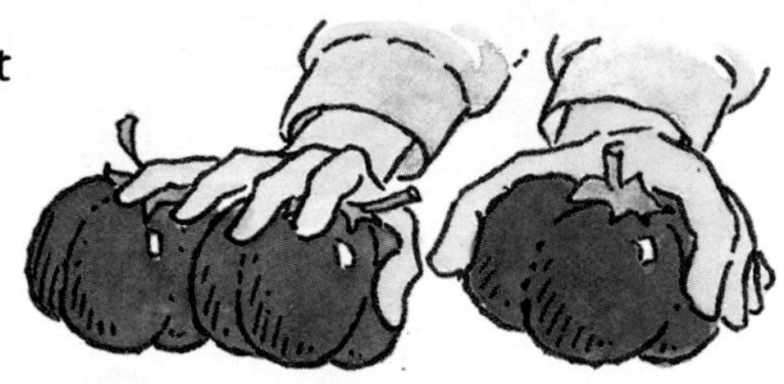

on the counter

on the shelf

on the stove

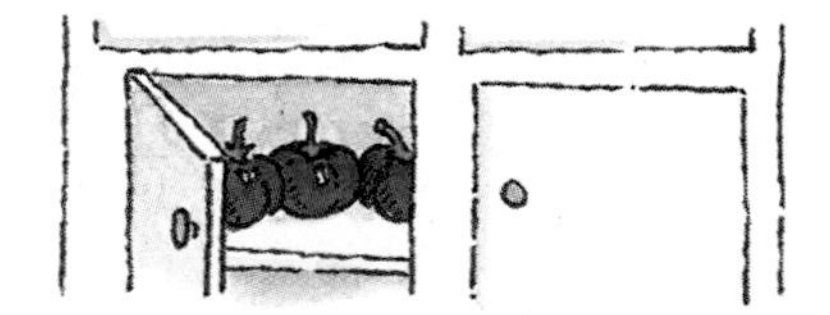

in the cabinet

in the refrigerator

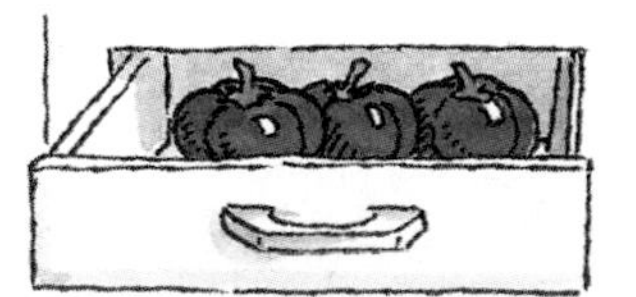

in the drawer

Listen and put your pictures in the correct places on your worksheet.

GROUP WORK

Make a group. Practice making requests like these. Use your worksheet.

Could you put the peppers in the refrigerator?
Sure.

Could you put the onion_________?
Sure.

Reading

Read these sentences and put your pictures in the correct places on your worksheet.

1. Put the tomato in the refrigerator.
2. Put the onions on the counter.
3. Put the tomatoes on the counter.
4. Put the eggs on the shelf.
5. Put the egg in the refrigerator.
6. Put the onion in the cabinet.

Writing

STEP ONE Complete these sentences (there are no wrong answers).

STEP TWO Read the directions to your classmates. They will put their pictures in the correct places on their worksheets.

1. Put the tomatoes ____.
2. Put the onion ____.
3. ____.
4. ____.
5. ____.
6. ____.

SITUATION B

Minh is visiting Maria. She's helping Maria cook.

Maria, where's the knife?
It's in the drawer.

Oh yeah. Here it is.

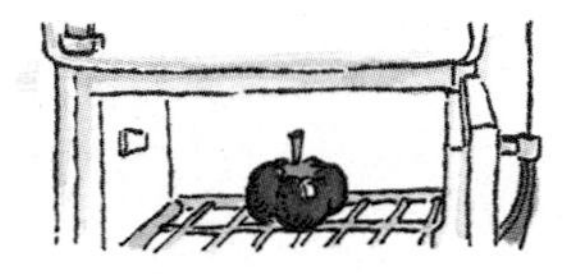

1. Where's the tomato?
   It's in the refrigerator.

2. Where are the tomatoes?
   They're in the refrigerator.

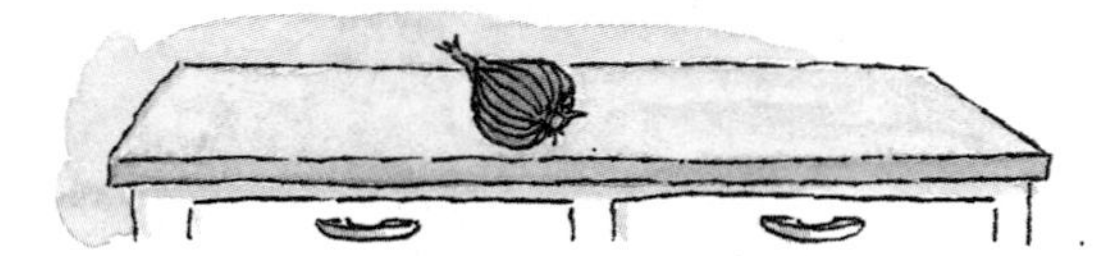

3. Where's the onion?
   It's on the counter.

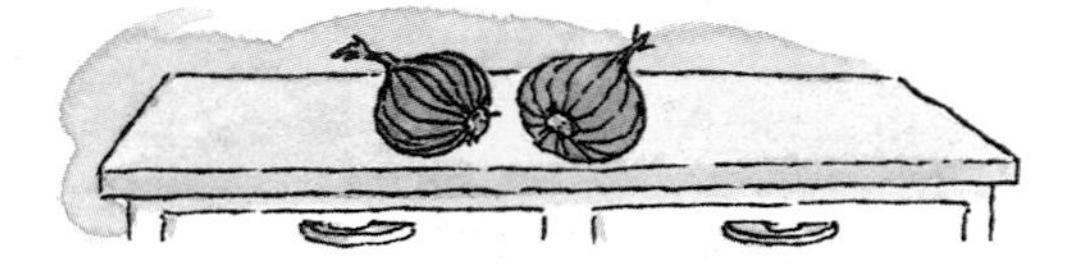

4. Where are the onions?
   They're on the counter.

Listen and put your pictures in the correct places on your worksheet.

GROUP WORK

Make a group. Practice asking questions. Use your worksheet.

Antonio, where are the tomatoes?
They're on the counter.

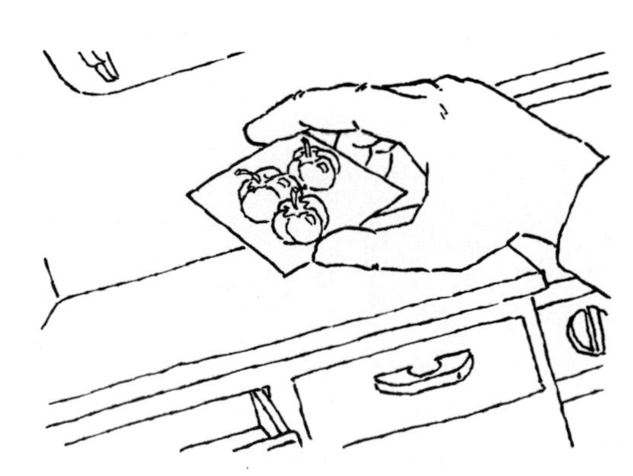

Reading

Read the story, and make a picture of Maria's kitchen with your worksheet. You can talk to your classmates about the story first.

MARIA'S KITCHEN

Maria has a big kitchen. She likes to cook. Right now, she's cooking Mexican-style eggs with her friend, Minh. She needs one tomato, three peppers, one onion, and six eggs. The tomato is in the refrigerator. The onion is in the cabinet. The eggs are in the refrigerator. The peppers are on the counter.

Maria needs a knife and a spoon, too. The knife is in the drawer. The spoon is on the shelf. The last thing she needs is a frying pan. The frying pan is on the stove.

Now clear your worksheet.

Writing

Think about your kitchen. Put your pictures on your worksheet. Write about your kitchen.

1. The knives are ______________________________.
2. The spoons are ______________________________.
3. The eggs are ______________________________.
4. ______________________________.
5. ______________________________.
6. ______________________________.
7. ______________________________.
8. ______________________________.

SITUATION

Minh and Maria are cooking.

	IS THE SPOON IN THE DRAWER?		ARE THE ONIONS ON THE COUNTER?	
Formal work, school 	Yes, it is. Yes.	No, it isn't. No.	Yes, they are. Yes.	No, they aren't. No.
Informal home, friends 	Yeah/Yup. Uh-huh.	Nah/Nope. Uh-uh.	Yeah/Yup. Uh-huh.	Nah/Nope. Uh-uh.

Listen and put your pictures in the correct places on your worksheet.

GROUP WORK

Take turns playing this game. Put one picture on your worksheet. Cover it. Your classmates will ask you questions to try to guess what your picture is and where your picture is on your worksheet.

Reading

Read this and write on the blanks below.

CHINESE FOOD

Maria is cooking Chinese food today. She's using a cookbook. She's reading a recipe. The recipe is for chicken with peppers and cabbage.

Maria is using a wok. A wok is a Chinese frying pan. She's also using a Chinese cleaver. A cleaver is a big knife.

Writing

Write the missing words.

1. Maria is cooking ________________ ________________.
2. She's reading ________ ________________.

SITUATION D

Minh is visiting Maria. Maria is making a salad.

Listen

Listen and circle the words you hear.

a knife

a spoon

three peppers

an onion

a tomato

a frying pan

an egg

three tomatoes

a bowl

a pepper

six eggs

three onions

GROUP WORK

Practice asking and answering questions. Use your worksheet.

Can I help?
Yes, thanks, Antonio. I need a knife.

Where is it?
It's ________.

Reading

Read this recipe for scrambled eggs. (This is for 2 or 3 people.)

1. Break 6 eggs into the bowl.

2. Cut up an onion, a pepper, and a tomato.
3. Put the onion, the pepper, and the tomato in the frying pan and cook.

4. Stir the eggs.

5. Put them in the frying pan and cook them.

Writing

Complete this recipe for a tomato salad.

INGREDIENTS

1. ______________________________
2. ______________________________
3. ______________________________

DIRECTIONS

1. ______________________________ the tomatoes, the onion, and the pepper.
2. ____________ the ingredients in a bowl.
3. ____________ the ingredients.

1\.

2\.

3\.

GRAMMAR CHECK

A. Singular/plural

Add **s** or **es** to regular nouns.

a tomato  three tomato**es**  an onion  three onion**s** 

B. Pronouns

The tomato	**is**	on	the counter.
			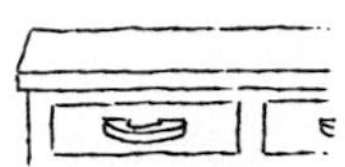
It	**is**	on	the counter.
		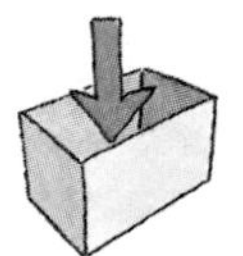	
The tomatoes	**are**	in	the refrigerator.
		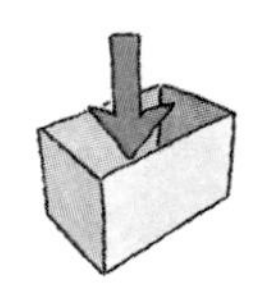	
They	**are**	in	the refrigerator.

C. Questions with *be*

			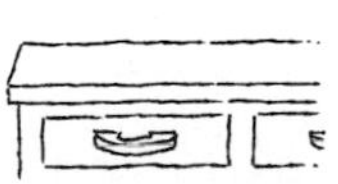
Is	the tomato	on	the counter?
			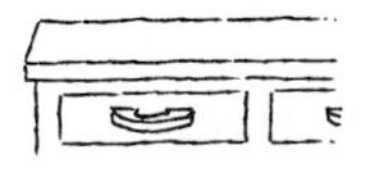
Are	the tomatoes	on	the counter?

YES/NO QUESTIONS AND ANSWERS WITH BE

<table>
<tr><td>Is</td><td>the onion
the tomato
the knife
the frying pan</td><td rowspan="2">in the cabinet
on the counter
in the drawer</td><td rowspan="2">?</td></tr>
<tr><td>Are</td><td>the onions
the tomatoes
the eggs
the peppers</td></tr>
</table>

Yes,	it is.
No,	it isn't.

Yes,	they are.
No,	they aren't.

• EXERCISE •

Look at the picture on page 13. Complete the story. Use **is** or **are.**

Maria ______is______ in the kitchen. The tomatoes ____________ on the counter in front of Maria. Maria ____________ cutting up the tomatoes with a knife. Minh ____________ in front of the refrigerator. She's putting away the eggs. Three peppers ____________ in the refrigerator, too, on the bottom shelf. The bowl ____________ on the top of the refrigerator. The frying pan ____________ on the stove. The two onions ____________ in the cabinet, behind Maria.

Maria and Minh ____________ making lunch. Maria ____________ making a salad.

Read the story to a partner. Your partner will put his/her pictures in the correct places on their worksheet.

ON YOUR OWN

Vocabulary

Do you know these words? Find them on page 13.

- ❑ kitchen
- ❑ bowl
- ❑ refrigerator
- ❑ eggs
- ❑ onion
- ❑ tomatoes
- ❑ drawer
- ❑ spoon
- ❑ knife
- ❑ counter
- ❑ bag
- ❑ egg
- ❑ stove
- ❑ tomato
- ❑ shelf
- ❑ frying pan
- ❑ peppers

Listening

Listen to your tape and put your pictures in the correct places on your worksheet. Then check your answer on page 13.

Minh: Where's the spoon?
Maria: It's in the drawer.
Minh: Oh, yeah. Now I need one pepper. Where is it?
Maria: The pepper?
Minh: Yeah.
Maria: It's on the counter, next to the refrigerator.

Maria: Hey, Minh, have you seen the onions?
Minh: Uh...I think they're in the cabinet.
Maria: Cabinet?
Minh: Yeah.
Maria: Oh yeah. Here they are.

Minh: Are the three peppers in the refrigerator?
Maria: Uh-huh.

Minh: O.K., now where's the bowl?
Maria: It's on the top of the refrigerator.
Minh: Oh yeah, here it is.

Minh: I need one more tomato. Is there one in the refrigerator?
Maria: No, but there is one on the shelf.
Minh: O.K., how about the frying pan?
Maria: It's on the stove.
Minh: Oh yeah. Here it is.

How to

tell someone "thank you"

CHAPTER 3

Time

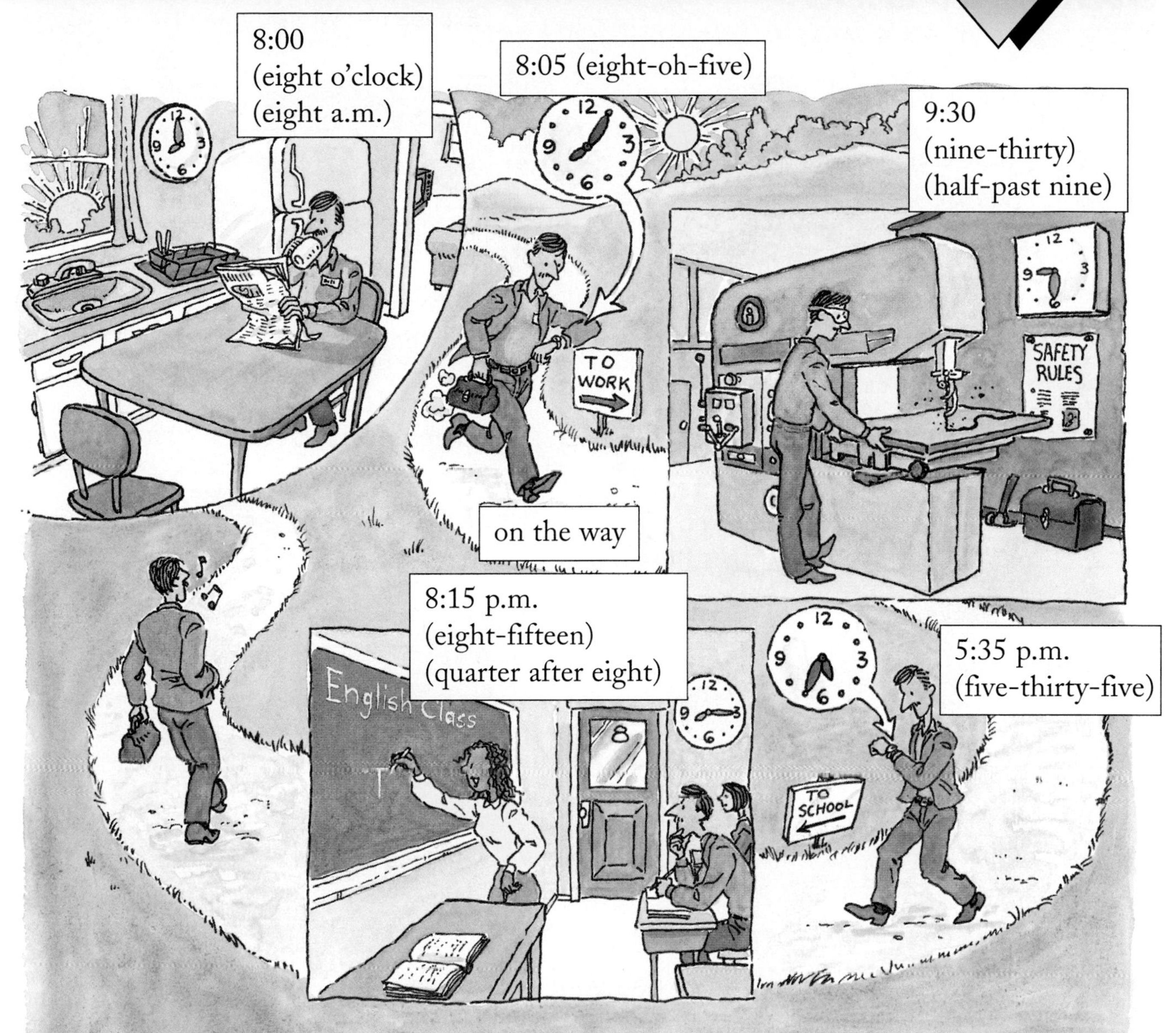

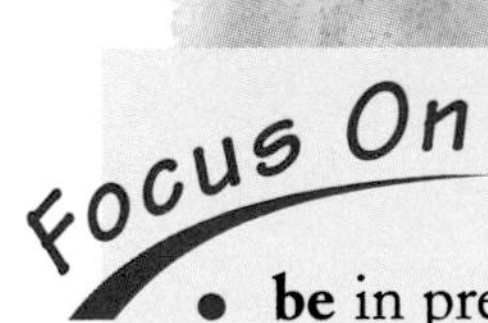

- **be** in present tense

  negative statements
- time vocabulary
- asking and telling the time

  "It's nine o'clock."
- describing location

  "He's at home."
- how to apologize

in the morning

in the afternoon

at night

SITUATION A

Bill is on his way to work. His job starts at 8:30.

Oh, no. I think I'm late.

Excuse me. What time is it?
It's 8:20.

Great! I'm not late.

Listen and put your pictures in the correct places on your worksheet.

GROUP WORK

Practice asking the time. Use your worksheet.

Excuse me. What time is it?
It's eight o'clock.

Reading

Read this, and put your pictures in the correct places on your worksheet.

IS HE LATE?

Bill's class starts at 6:30. It's 6:35 right now. Bill is on the way to school. He's late. Suzy isn't late. She's at school.

Now cover the reading, and look at your picture. What can you remember about the story?

Writing

Fill in the missing words.

Bill's class ________________ at 6:30. It's 6:35 right now. Bill is

________________ ________________ ________________ to school.

He's ________________. Suzy ________________ late.

She's at school.

Now clear your worksheet.

Put your pictures on your worksheet. What time is it? Where is Bill? Where is Suzy? Then complete the sentences. There are no wrong or right answers.

It's ________________ right now. Bill is ______________________.

Suzy is ______________________.

Read your story to your classmates. They will put their pictures in the correct places on their worksheets.

S I T U A T I O N

A busy day for Bill and Suzy.

1. It's eight A.M. Bill is at home. Suzy isn't at home. She's on the way to work.

2. It's 11:00 A.M. Bill isn't at home now. He's at work. Suzy is on the way to school.

3. It's eight P.M. Bill isn't at work now. He's on the way home. Suzy is at school.

4. It's 11:00 P.M. Bill is at home. Suzy is at home, too.

Listen and put your pictures in the correct places on your worksheet.

Practice talking about Bill and Suzy. Use your worksheet.

It's nine A.M.
Suzy isn't at home.
She's at work.

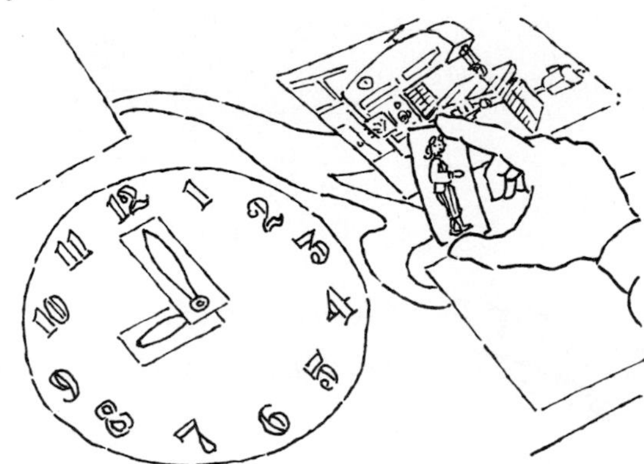

Reading/Writing

Read this and then label the picture below.

Suzy's Favorite Time

It's eight o'clock in the morning. Suzy is at home. This is her favorite time of the day. She's sitting in her favorite chair, a big armchair. The chair is in front of the window, and the sun is shining outside. She's reading the newspaper. She's drinking a big cup of coffee. She's happy. This is her favorite time.

Extra *Write about your favorite time. What time is it? What are you doing?*

SITUATION C

A TV reporter is asking questions.

Listen

Listen and put your pictures in the correct places on your worksheet.

GROUP WORK

Practice asking and answering questions like these.

Reading

Read about Bill and Suzy. Put your pictures in the correct places on your worksheet.

It's nine o'clock in the morning. I'm usually at work, but I'm not at work today. It's a holiday. I'm at home.

It's nine A.M. I'm usually at school at this time, but I'm not there right now. I'm really late today. I'm on my way to school.

Writing

Write about where you are at these times.

1. At 9:00 in the morning, I'm ______________________________.

2. At 5:30 in the afternoon, ______________________________.

3. At 1:30 P.M. ______________________________.

4. At 11:00 A.M. ______________________________.

5. ______________________________.

6. ______________________________.

7. ______________________________.

SITUATION D

The English class begins at 6:30 P.M.

Lisa is very early. She's not late.

Mike is a little early. He's not late.

Ann is right on time. She's not late.

Bob is a little late.

Sylvie is very late.

Listen

Listen and put your pictures in the correct places on your worksheet.

Is Bill Late?

A party begins at 9:00 P.M.

Bill arrives at 9:20.

GROUP WORK

What do you think? Is Bill on time, early, late, a little late, or very late? Talk to your group.

He's late. He's very late.
He's not late. He's on time.
He's ____.

Reading

WHAT IS LATE?

Different people have different ideas about time. If a party starts at 9:00 P.M., some people arrive at exactly 9:00 P.M. Other people arrive at 9:15 P.M. Still other people arrive at 10:00 P.M., or even 11:00 P.M. What is late? What about you? What do you think?

If a party starts at 9:00 P.M., I arrive at __________.

Writing

Do a survey. Ask 5 people this question, and write their answers below.

A party starts at 9:00 P.M. When do you arrive in your country?

	name	*country*	*time*
1.			
2.			
3.			
4.			
5.			

Talk about your surveys with your classmates. Are the times different?

GRAMMAR CHECK

The Negative of *be*

The negative word is **not:**

I **am** **not** late.

The contraction looks like this:

I**'m** **not** late.

Third person singular looks like this:

He **is** not late.

She **is** **not** late.

There are two contractions:

He**'s** **not** late.

She**'s** **not** late.

He **isn't** late.

She **isn't** late.

Here are some other contractions:

they**'re** **not**

they **aren't**

we**'re** **not**

we **aren't**

you**'re** **not**

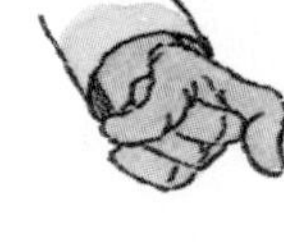 

you **aren't**

TIME QUESTIONS AND ANSWERS WITH **BE**

What time	is	it?

It	is 's	ten A.M. ten o'clock. eleven-fifteen.

AFFIRMATIVE AND NEGATIVE STATEMENTS WITH **BE**

I	am 'm am not 'm not	at home. at school. at work. on the way home. on the way to work. on the way to school.
He She	is 's isn't 's not	
You We They	are 're aren't 're not	

•EXERCISE•

Look at page 25. Complete these sentences about the picture. Write **He's** or **He isn't.**

1. It's eight o'clock in the morning. Bill is at home.

   He isn't at work yet.

2. It's 8:05. He's on the way to work. __________ at home now.

3. It's 9:30. __________ at work. __________ at school.

4. It's 5:35 P.M. __________ not at work now.

   __________ on the way to school.

5. It's 8:15 P.M. __________ on his way home yet.

   __________ at school.

Extra *Write as many sentences as you can about the picture on page 25.*

ON YOUR OWN

Vocabulary

Do you know these words? Find them on page 25.

- ❑ 8:00 (eight o'clock)
- ❑ 8:15 (eight fifteen)
- ❑ 9:30 (nine thirty)
- ❑ 5:15 (five fifteen)
- ❑ 6:00 (six o'clock)
- ❑ 9:09 (nine-oh-nine)
- ❑ home
- ❑ work
- ❑ school
- ❑ class
- ❑ way
- ❑ A.M.
- ❑ P.M.
- ❑ early
- ❑ right on time
- ❑ late

Listening

Listen to your tape and put your pictures in the correct places on your worksheet. Then check your answer on page 25.

A.

Bill: Excuse me, Sir. Do you have the time?

Man: Ummmm.... I think it's about five-thirty-five.

Bill: Thank you.

Announcer: It's five-thirty-five in the afternoon, and Bill is on his way to school.

B.

Bill: Suzy, do you know what time it is?

Suzy: Eight o'clock.

Bill: Thanks.

Announcer: It's eight o'clock in the morning, and Bill is at home.

C.

Bill: Hey, Maria, do you know what time it is?

Maria: Yes. It's exactly six o'clock.

Announcer: It's six P.M., and Bill is in class.

D.

Bill: Pardon me, ma'am. What time is it?

Woman: It's eight-oh-five.

Bill: Thank you very much.

Announcer: It's eight-oh-five in the morning, and Bill is on his way to work.

E.

Bill: Excuse me, Charlie. What time is it?

Charlie: Uh, let's see . . . It's nine-thirty.

Announcer: It's nine-thirty A.M. Bill is at work.

How to
apologize to someone

A Restaurant

CHAPTER 4

Focus On

- count/non-count nouns
- restaurant and food vocabulary
- asking for and giving prices
  "How much?"
- asking about and describing the condition of something
  "How's the soup?"
- requests with *"I'd like"*
- how to clarify a price

SITUATION 

Al is at a catering truck.

Hi.
Hi. Can I help you?
ACME CATERING
ACME CATERING
How much is a hamburger?
A dollar eighty.

$1.69

$.50

	How much is a sandwich?	How much is a soda?
Formal	It's one dollar and sixty-nine cents.	It's fifty cents.
Informal	It's a dollar sixty-nine. One sixty-nine. A buck sixty-nine.	Fifty cents.

Listen and put your pictures in the correct places on your worksheet.

GROUP WORK

Practice asking and answering questions. Put your pictures in the correct places on your worksheet.

How much is a hamburger?
It's a dollar fifteen.
WORKSHEET

Reading

Read this and put your pictures in the correct places on your worksheet.

JOE'S RESTAURANT

Joe's Restaurant is very good. It's my favorite place for lunch. It's across the street from my school. The prices are excellent. A hamburger is only $1.30, and a big salad is only $1.50. They have very good french fries. The french fries are only $1.25 for a big order. Coffee is 50 cents.

Writing

______________________ RESTAURANT

9039

Step One Make a group. This is your restaurant. Give it a name.
Step Two Decide prices.

1. The name of my restaurant is ______________________
2. A hamburger is ______________________
3. ______________________
4. ______________________
5. ______________________
6. ______________________

Read your sentences to the class. Your classmates will put their pictures in the correct places on their worksheets.

S I T U A T I O N B

Al is at a restaurant.

Good morning.
(Hello.)

noon–6 P.M.
Good afternoon.
(Hello.)

6 P.M.–midnight
Good evening.
(Hello.)

Listen and put your pictures in the correct places on your worksheet.

GROUP WORK

Make a group. One student is the waiter or waitress. The other students order. Use your pictures.

Anything else?

Yes, a cup of coffee, please.

Good evening. Are you ready to order?

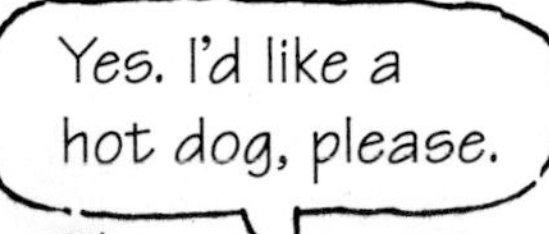

Reading

Read this and put your pictures in the correct places on your worksheet.

MY FAVORITE RESTAURANT

My favorite restaurant is in downtown Chicago. They have wonderful hamburgers. They're only $1.50. The hot dogs are very good, too. They're cheap—only a dollar fifteen! The coffee is excellent and it's only forty-five cents. The best thing is the pie. They have delicious apple pie. It's only $1.25.

Writing

Write about your favorite restaurant.

MY FAVORITE RESTAURANT

My name is ______________________________.
(*name*)

My favorite restaurant is ______________________________.
(*name of restaurant*)

It's in ______________________________. They
(*city or country*)

have wonderful ______________. ______________
(*food*)

____

____.

Work with your classmates. Make a guidebook about your classmates' favorite restaurants. Share your book with the school.

SITUATION 

Oscar and Linda are talking about food prices in their countries.

He's from China.

She's from Colombia.

Listen

Listen and put your pictures in the correct places on your worksheet.

GROUP WORK

Make a group. Practice asking and answering questions about food prices in your town or country.

Reading

Read this and then write the prices below.

POOR AL

Al is from Elk City, Oklahoma. He lives in Los Angeles now. The prices are high in Los Angeles. Food is cheaper in Elk City. Coffee is fifty cents in Elk City. But it's seventy-five cents in Los Angeles. A hamburger is only $1.30 in Elk City. But in Los Angeles, a hamburger is $1.90. A salad is seventy-five cents in Elk City. In Los Angeles, it's $1.80. Al loves pie. A piece of pie in Elk City is sixty cents. In Los Angeles, a piece of pie is $1.50.

ELK CITY	
coffee	.50¢
a hamburger	______
a salad	______
pie	______

LOS ANGELES	
coffee	.75¢
a hamburger	______
a salad	______
pie	______

Writing

Write about the prices of food in your country.

I'm from ______________________________.

1. In my country, a cup of coffee is ______________________________.
2. In my country, a ______________________________.
3. ______________________________.
4. ______________________________.
5. ______________________________.

SITUATION

Pam is at a restaurant.

IS
The soup is very good.
The salad is very good.
The tea is very good.
The pie is very good.
The ice cream is very good.
The soda is very good.
The coffee is very good.

ARE
The hamburgers are very good.
The hot dogs are very good.
The sandwiches are very good.
The french fries are very good.

Listen and put your pictures in the correct places on your worksheet.

GROUP WORK

Practice asking and answering questions like these. Use your worksheet.

What's good?
The soup is very good today. It's excellent.
How much is a bowl of soup?
_______________.

Writing

Step One Make a group and write a short play. Your actors are a waiter and a customer.

Step Two Act out the play for your class.

Waiter: Good ______________________. Are you ready to order?

Customer: ____.

Waiter: ____.

Customer: ____.

Waiter: ____.

Customer: ____.

Waiter: ____.

Customer: ____.

Waiter: ____.

Customer: ____.

Waiter: ____.

Customer: ____.

Waiter: ____.

Customer: ____.

Waiter: ____.

Customer: ____.

Waiter: ____.

Customer: ____.

Waiter: ____.

GRAMMAR CHECK

Count and non-count nouns

Some things we can count. They are singular or plural.

I want a hamburger, please.

The hamburgers are very good.

Some things we can't count. They are always singular.

But we can count bowls of soup.

I'd like a bowl of chicken soup, please.

I'd like two bowls of chicken soup, please.

Make a list of foods you know. Put them in column 1 or column 2.

Count Nouns	***Non-count Nouns***
The ____________ are very good.	The ____________ is very good.
________________________________.	________________________________.
________________________________.	________________________________.
________________________________.	________________________________.
________________________________.	________________________________.

QUESTIONS AND ANSWERS WITH **HOW MUCH?**

How much	is	a cup of coffee a piece of pie a bowl of soup	?
	are	the hamburgers the hot dogs	

It's	fifty cents. a dollar fifty. one dollar and ten cents.
They're	

NON-COUNT NOUNS (SINGULAR ONLY)

The coffee The pie The soup The salad	is 's	great. very good. good. fresh. fifty cents. a dollar fifty. one-fifteen.

COUNT NOUNS (SINGULAR OR PLURAL)

The restaurant The hot dog	is	great. good. very good. fresh. fifty cents. a dollar-fifty. one-fifteen.
The hamburgers The apples The sandwiches	are	

•EXERCISE•

Complete these sentences. Use **is** or **are.**

1. How much ___is___ a hot dog?
2. The hot dogs __________ very good today. Would you like one?
3. How much __________ a hamburger?
4. The hamburgers __________ more expensive than the pizza.
5. The coffee __________ too hot to drink.
6. How much __________ a soda?
7. The pie __________ very good.
8. How much __________ a piece of pie?
9. The apples __________ sour. Would you like an orange?

ON YOUR OWN

Vocabulary

Do you know these words? Find them on page 37.

- ❑ a restaurant
- ❑ waiter
- ❑ a hot dog
- ❑ a soda
- ❑ a piece of pie
- ❑ a sandwich
- ❑ an order of french fries
- ❑ a bowl of ice cream
- ❑ waitress
- ❑ a bowl of soup
- ❑ a hamburger
- ❑ a menu
- ❑ a salad
- ❑ a cup of tea
- ❑ a cup of coffee
- ❑ a slice of pizza
- ❑ customer

Listening

Listen to your tape and put your pictures in the correct places on your worksheet. Then check your answer on page 37.

Al: Excuse me, how much is a slice of pizza?

Waitress: Uh. . . . a dollar-thirty. Would you like one?

Al: Yes, and something else . . . maybe the soup?

Waitress: The soup is excellent today, and it's only seventy-five cents. Anything to drink?

Al: How much is a cup of coffee?

Waitress: Forty-five cents, and refills are free.

Al: Ok. I'll take coffee.

Waitress: What about you, miss? I see you already have a hamburger on your plate. Can I get you anything else?

Pam: Hmm . . . maybe I should get a salad. The menu says it's on special . . .

Waitress: Yes, it's a dollar-fifty today.

Pam: That's great. And I'll have a cup of tea, too. That's fifty cents, right?

Waitress: Uh-huh. I'll go get it for you now.

How to
clarify a price

CHAPTER 

Your Neighborhood

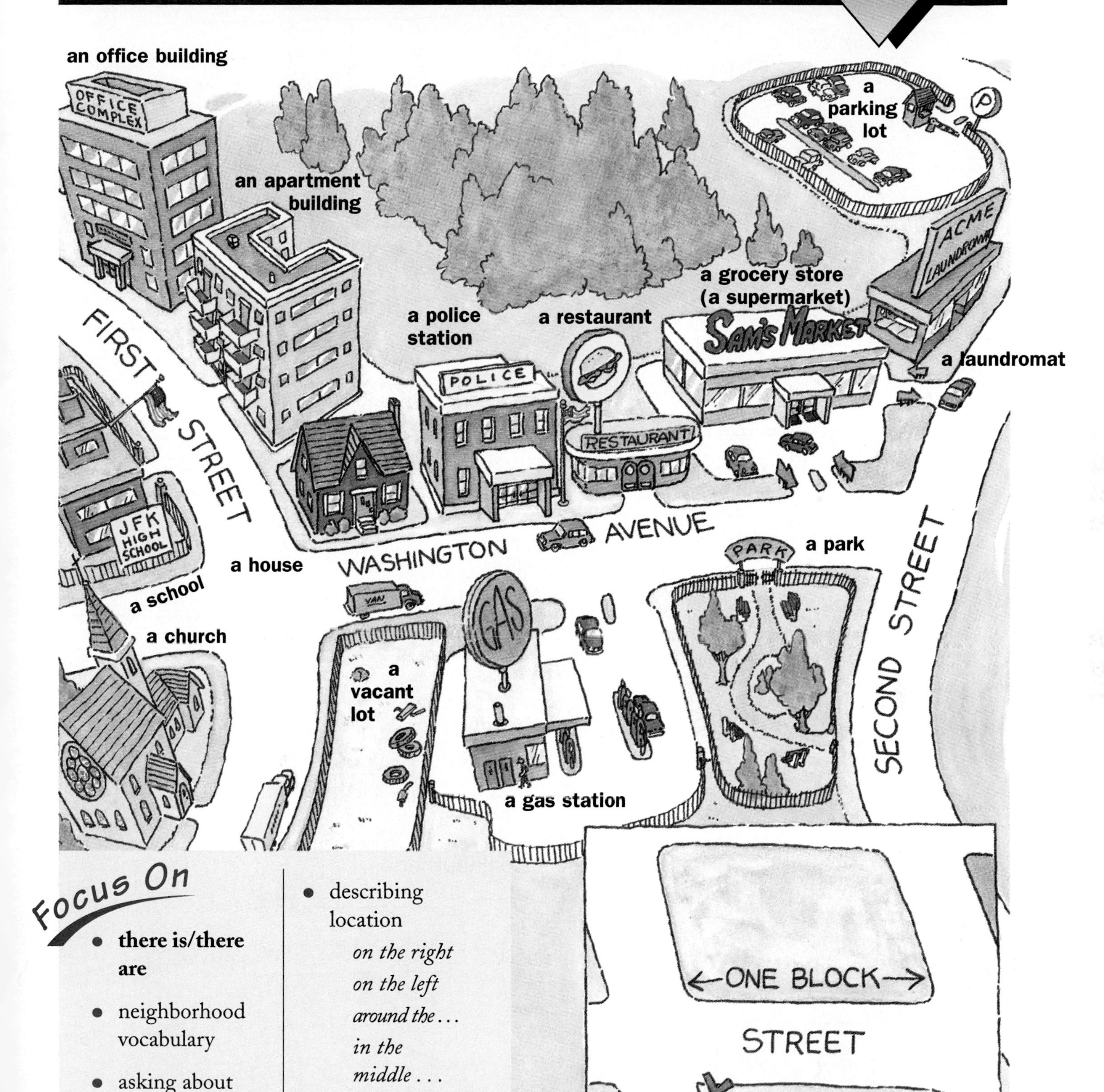

Focus On

- **there is/there are**
- neighborhood vocabulary
- asking about the existence of a place
  "Is there a . . . "
- describing location
  on the right
  on the left
  around the . . .
  in the middle . . .
- how to get someone's attention

SITUATION A

Jon is describing his neighborhood.

I live in an apartment building on Washington Avenue. It's in the middle of the block.
WASHINGTON AVENUE
FIRST STREET
WASHINGTON AVENUE
WASHINGTON AVENUE
SECOND STREET

It's on the corner of First Street and Washington Avenue.

It's on the corner of Second Street and Washington Avenue.

Listen

Listen and put your pictures in the correct places on your worksheet.

GROUP WORK

Practice describing an imaginary neighborhood.

I live in a house on Washington Avenue. It's on the corner of Second Street.

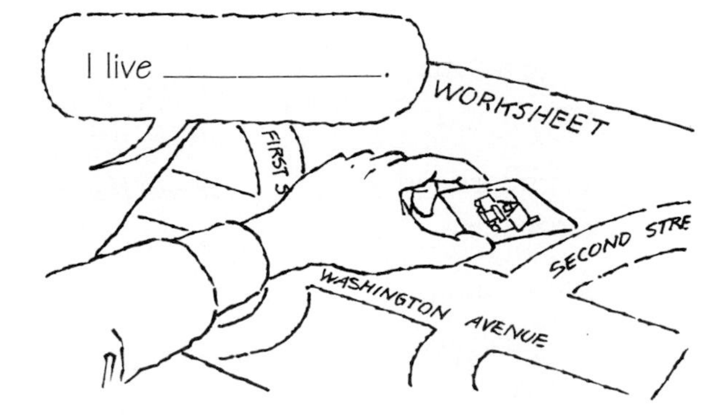

I live ________.
WORKSHEET
FIRST S
SECOND STRE
WASHINGTON AVENUE

Reading

Read this, and put your pictures in the correct places on your worksheet.

I live in a small house on Washington Avenue. It's on the corner of Second Street. Next to my house, on the left, there's a parking lot. Next to the parking lot, there's a gas station.

Clear your worksheet. Now read this.

I live in an apartment building on Washington Avenue. It's in the middle of the block. Next to my apartment building, on the right, there's a police station. Next to the police station, there's a school.

Now clear your worksheet again.

Writing

Write about your street.

I live in ____
(a house / an apartment building)

on ____. On the right of my
(name of your street)

______________________________ there is ______________________________
(house / apartment building)

______________. Next to that is a ______________________________.

Extra *Read your story to the class or your group. They will put their pictures in the correct places on their worksheets.*

SITUATION

Jon and Becky are talking.

Do you live in an apartment building or a house?
A house. On the corner of Washington and First.
It's a great block. I love it.
How come?
Across the street from my house, there's a big park.
FIRST STREET
WASHINGTON AVENUE
PARK
And around the corner there's a supermarket. It's perfect.
SAM'S MARKET
FIRST STREET
WASHINGTON

Listen

Listen and put your pictures in the correct places on your worksheet.

GROUP WORK

Work together. Make a neighborhood. Use your worksheet.

There's a parking lot on the corner of Washington and Second.
There's a small house around the corner from the parking lot.

Reading

Read this, and put your pictures in the correct places on your worksheet.

MY BLOCK

Here is a map of my block. My apartment building is in the middle of the block. It's on Washington Avenue. Next to my apartment building, on the right, there's a Mexican restaurant. It's very good. I eat there a lot.

Next to my apartment building, on the left, there's a laundromat. I do my laundry at the laundromat. It's very convenient. Next to the laundromat, on the corner, there's a parking lot. There's a big office building across the street from the parking lot.

Writing

Write about your block.

1. I live in ______________________________.
(a house / an apartment building)

2. On the right side of my ______________________________
(house / apartment building)

there's ______________________________.

3. On the left side of my ______________________________
(house / apartment building)

there's ______________________________.

4. Across the street from my ______________________________,
(house / apartment)

there's ______________________________.

5. ______________________________

______________________________.

SITUATION C

Jon is looking for a laundromat.

Is there a	laundromat gas station parking lot church police station	in this neighborhood? nearby? around here?

Listen and put your pictures in the correct places on your worksheet.

GROUP WORK

Make a group. Practice asking questions. Use your worksheet.

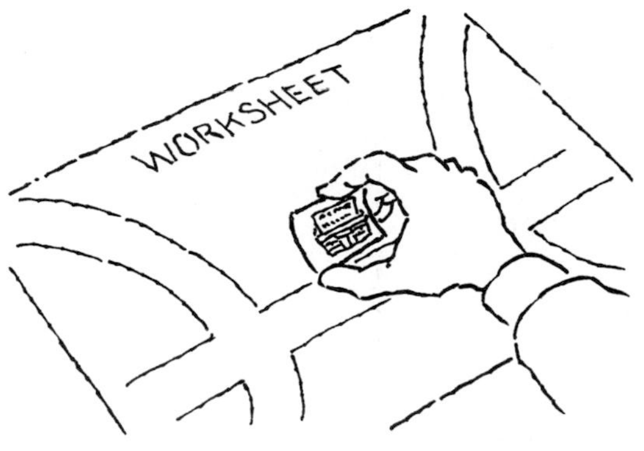

Reading

Read this, and put your pictures in the correct places on your worksheet.

My Neighborhood

My neighborhood is nice. I live in a big apartment building in the middle of a busy block. There aren't any problems with crime because there's a police station next to my apartment building, on the left. Next to the police station, there's a big Catholic church. I go there on Sunday. There aren't any gas stations in my neighborhood, but that's OK because I don't have a car.

There's only one problem in my neighborhood—there's a parking lot across the street from my apartment building, and it's very busy. All those cars make a lot of noise!

Writing

Address this letter to your school. Put your return address in the top left corner.

____
(your name)

____
(your address)

____
(your city, state, and zip code)

____
(name of your school)

____
(address of your school)

____
(city, state, and zip code)

SITUATION

D

Jeff and Ana are looking for an apartment

This neighborhood is nice.
Yes, but there aren't any laundromats. We need a laundromat nearby.
FOR RENT

That's true. But it's very quiet.
There aren't any schools around here, either.

We need a school, and we need a laundromat nearby.
Yeah. I guess you're right.

There aren't any	parks. parking lots. factories. churches. houses.

Listen

Listen and put your pictures in the correct places on your worksheet.

GROUP WORK

Talk about your neighborhood. Use your worksheet.

I live in an apartment building.
On the corner?

No, in the middle of the block. Next to my apartment building, there's a ____.

Reading

Read this, and put your pictures in the correct places on your worksheet.

MY PERFECT BLOCK

I'd like to live in a big house in the middle of the block. I'd like a park on the right side of my house. Next to the park, on the corner, I'd like a gas station. I'd like a laundromat on the left side of my house. Next to the laundromat, on the other corner, I'd like a supermarket.

Writing

Complete these sentences about your perfect neighborhood.

1. I'd like to live in ______________________________ in the middle of the block.
2. I'd like ______________________________
   on the right side of my ______________________________.
3. Next to the ______________________________ I'd like
   ______________________________, on the corner.
4. I'd like ______________________________
   on the left side of my ______________________________.
5. Next to the ______________________________ I'd like
   ______________________________, on the other corner.
6. ______________________________
   ______________________________.

Read your story to your group or to the class. They will put their pictures in the correct places on their worksheets.

GRAMMAR CHECK

There is / there are

When we describe places we often use **there is** or **there are:**

There	**is**	a church	in	my neighborhood.

When we speak, we usually make a contraction:

There'**s**	a church	in	my neighborhood.

Two or more things use **are:**

			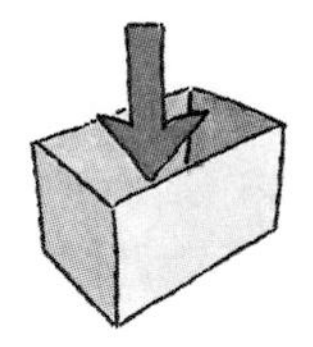	
There	**are**	two churches	in	my neighborhood.

Here's how we use **not** to make negative statements.

There	is**n't**	a church	in	my neighborhood.

There	are**n't**	any churches	in	my neighborhood.

THERE IS / THERE ARE

AFFIRMATIVE STATEMENTS

There is There's	a church a parking lot a park	on the right corner. on the left corner. around the corner. next to my house.
There are	two churches three houses	

NEGATIVE STATEMENTS

There isn't There's not	a church a parking lot a park	in this neighborhood. around here.
There aren't	any churches any houses any parks	

YES / NO QUESTIONS AND ANSWERS

Is there	a church a parking lot	around here	?
Are there	any stores any gas stations		

Yes, there is.	No, there isn't.
Yes, there are.	No, there aren't.

•EXERCISE•

Look at the picture on page 49. Fill in the blanks in this story about the picture. Use **there is**, **there are**, or **there aren't** (any).

1. There is ______ a house next to the police station.
2. ______ ten cars in the parking lot.
3. ______ four trees in the park.
4. ______ an apartment building around the corner from the house.
5. ______ any cars in the vacant lot.
6. ______ a grocery store across from the park.
7. ______ any people in the vacant lot.
8. ______ a high school on the corner of First Street and Washington Avenue.
9. ______ two cars at the grocery store.
10. ______ a laundromat next to the grocery store, on the right.

ON YOUR OWN

Vocabulary

Do you know these words? Find them on page 49.

- ❑ an office building
- ❑ an apartment building
- ❑ a school
- ❑ a house
- ❑ a police station
- ❑ a restaurant
- ❑ a grocery store
- ❑ a laundromat
- ❑ a parking lot
- ❑ a vacant lot
- ❑ a church
- ❑ a gas station
- ❑ a park
- ❑ one block
- ❑ street
- ❑ corner

Listening

Listen to your tape, and put your pictures in the correct places on your worksheet. Then check your answer on page 49.

Becky: My neighborhood is nice. I live in a small house. It's on the corner of Washington and First. Next to my house, on the right, there's a police station. There's a restaurant next to the police station. Around the corner from my house, there's an apartment building. It's a big apartment building.

Across from my house, there's a vacant lot, right on the corner. Next to the vacant lot, there's a big gas station. On the corner of Second Street, next to the gas station, there's a park. On the other corner of my block, across from the park, there's a grocery store. Around the corner from the store, there's a laundromat.

How to
get the attention of a stranger

Excuse me, sir.
Yes?
Excuse me, ma'am.
Yes?

CHAPTER 6

At Work, at Home, and on Vacation

Focus On

- present continuous tense
- work, home, and vacation vocabulary
- giving instructions
  "Put the box in the truck."
- describing the location and activity of yourself and others
  "I'm at work."
  "I'm at home."
- how to tell someone you're busy

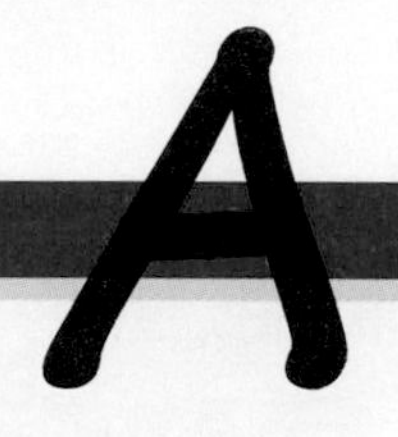

S I T U A T I O N A

Joe is talking to the boss.

<table>
<tr><td rowspan="2">Put it</td><td>on</td><td>the loading dock,
the first floor,
the second floor,
the third floor,</td><td rowspan="2">please.</td></tr>
<tr><td>in</td><td>the truck,
the warehouse,
the employee lounge,</td></tr>
</table>

Listen and put your pictures in the correct places on your worksheet.

GROUP • WORK •

Practice asking and answering questions. Use your worksheet.

Where do you want the red box?
Put it in the office, please.

Reading

Read this memo, and put your pictures in the correct places on your worksheet.

> ***MEMO***
>
> To: Caroline
>
> From: Mr. Smith
>
> There are three boxes in the truck. Unload them. Put the green box on the first floor, in the warehouse. Put the blue one on the second floor. The red box goes in the office, next to the desk. Thanks.

Writing

Write a memo. Then read it to the class. They will put their pictures in the correct places on their worksheets.

> ***MEMO***
>
> To: The class
>
> From:
>
> 1. Put the green box ______________________________
>
> ______________________________.
>
> 2. Put the red one ______________________________
>
> ______________________________.
>
> 3. The blue one goes ______________________________
>
> ______________________________.

Close your book and write another memo.

SITUATION B

The boss is asking about Kim.

Hey, Sam?
Yes, Mr. Smith?
COLA

Is Kim at work today?
Yes. She's on the assembly line.

1. Is Miguel at work today?
Yes, he's on the loading dock.

2. Is Caroline at work today?
No, she's sick today.
She's at home.

3. Is Joe at work today?
No, he's on vacation.

Listen and put your pictures in the correct places on your worksheet.

GROUP WORK

Practice asking and answering questions. Use your worksheets.

Is Gina at work today?
Yes. She's in the employee lounge.

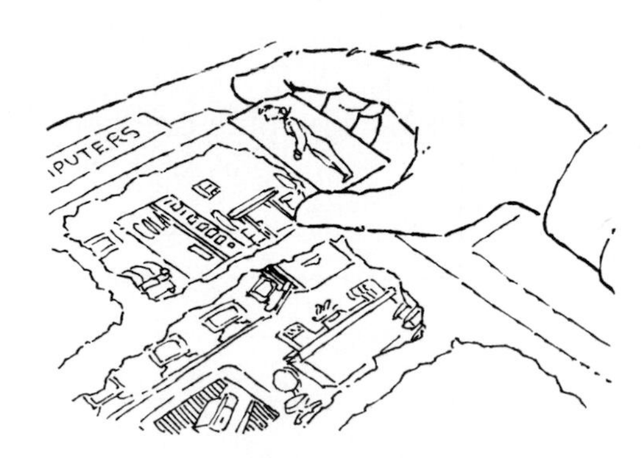

Reading

Read this, and put your pictures in the correct places on your worksheet.

Today is a busy day at the Acme Computer Company. Sam is at work. He's in the office right now. Kim is at work, too. She's on the second floor, on the assembly line. Joe's on the third floor, in the employee lounge. Miguel's on the first floor. He's in the warehouse.

Caroline isn't at work today. She's at home, in bed. She's sick. Gina's not at work, either, but she's not at home. She's on vacation. She's at the beach.

Now clear your worksheet.

Writing

Complete these sentences. There are no right or wrong answers.

1. Sam ______________________ at work today.

He's ______________________.

2. Kim ______________________ at work today.

She's ______________________.

3. Joe ______________________ at work today.

He's ______________________.

4. Caroline ______________________ at work today.

She's ______________________.

5. Gina ______________________

______________________.

6. Miguel ______________________

______________________.

SITUATION C

Kim and Caroline are talking about Sam.

Where's Sam? Is he sick today?

Oh, that's right. He's in Mexico. He's lying on the beach right now.
Yeah. Lucky guy!

He's	talking to the secretary. taking a break. working on the assembly line. moving boxes.
She's	loading a truck. sick. lying on the beach.

Listen and put your pictures in the correct places on your worksheet.

GROUP WORK

Practice asking and answering questions. Use your worksheet.

Where's Sam?
He's at home. He's sick.

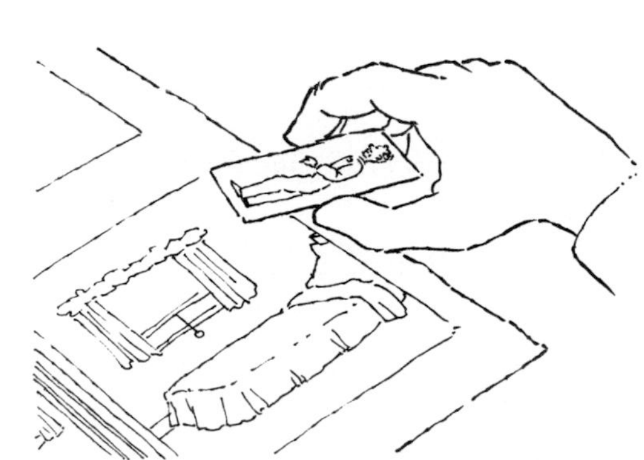

Reading 

Read this, and put your pictures in the correct places on your worksheet.

The Acme Company

Mr. Smith is the boss at the Acme Computer Company. He has a lot of problems today. Two people are sick—Gina and Caroline are at home. Joe is on vacation this week. Sam usually works in the warehouse on the first floor, but today he's working on the assembly line. Miguel and Kim are working on the assembly line, too.

Sam is putting the memory chips in the computer. Miguel is assembling the two pieces of the case. And Kim is putting in the screws.

Match the phrases and the pictures.

assembling the two pieces of the case

putting memory chips in the computer

putting in the screws

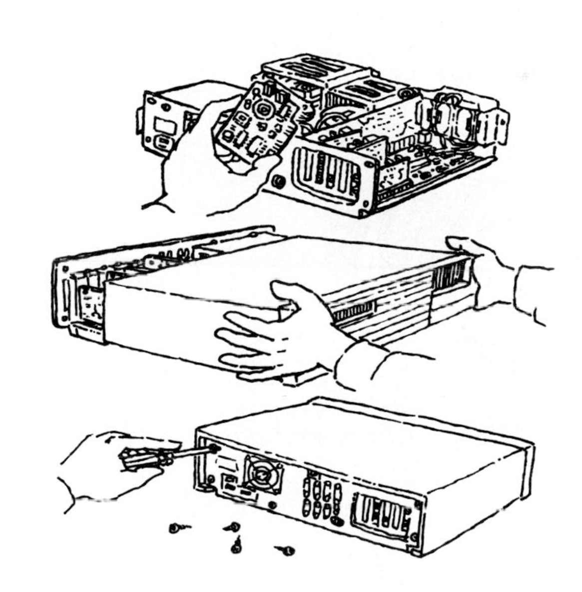

Writing 

What are they doing in the reading above? Complete the sentences.

1. Miguel is ______________________________.
2. Kim is ______________________________.
3. Sam is ______________________________.

SITUATION D

Mr. Smith is talking on the intercom.

Listen and put your pictures in the correct places on your worksheet.

GROUP • WORK •

Practice asking and answering questions. Use your worksheet.

Hey, Caroline. What are you doing?

I'm working on the assembly line.

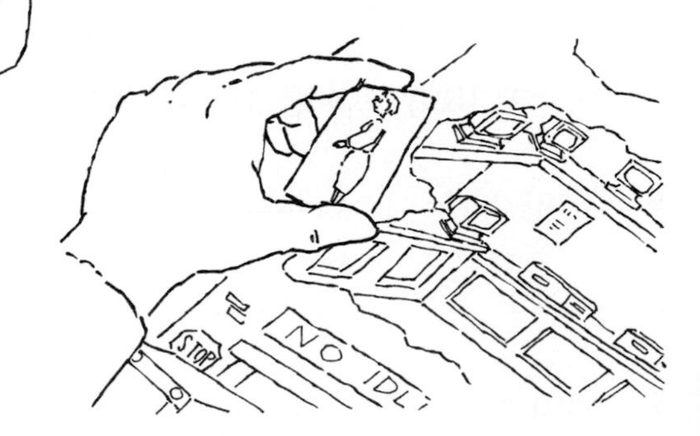

Reading

Read this chart, and put your pictures in the correct places on your worksheet.

IT'S 10:01 A.M. WHERE IS EVERYBODY?

NAME	1ST BREAK	2ND BREAK	JOB SITE
1. Kim	10:00	3:00	assembly line
2. Joe	10:30	2:30	assembly line
3. Caroline	11:00	4:00	loading dock
4. Sam			on vacation
5. Gina			day off
6. Miguel	10:00	3:00	warehouse

Writing

Write about the Acme Computer Company. Use the chart above.

It's 10:01 A.M.

1. Kim is at work today. She's taking a break right now. ______________.

2. ____.

3. ____.

4. ____.

5. ____.

6. ____.

7. ____.

GRAMMAR CHECK

Present continuous tense

If an action is happening right now, we use the present continuous tense.

Joe

is

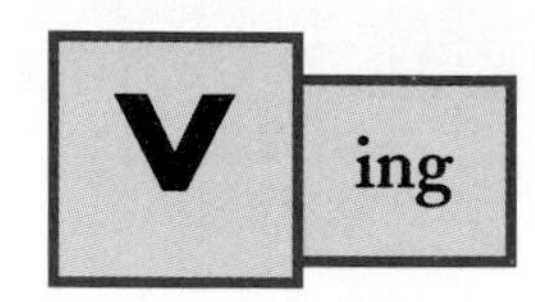

loading

a truck.

This is the base form of a verb.
A verb is usually an action.

load

We make the continuous form when we add **-ing.**

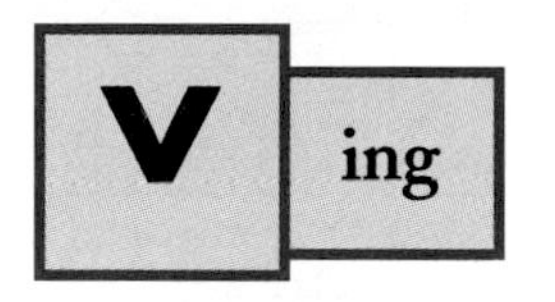

load**ing**

We use **be** + **base form** + **-ing** to make the present continuous tense.

I

am

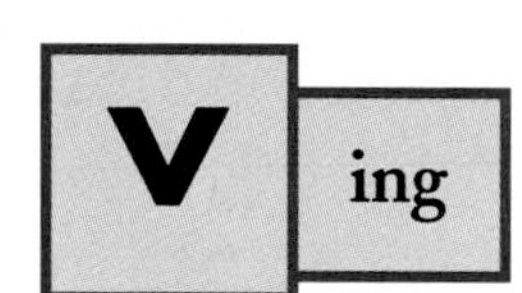

sleep**ing.**

She

is

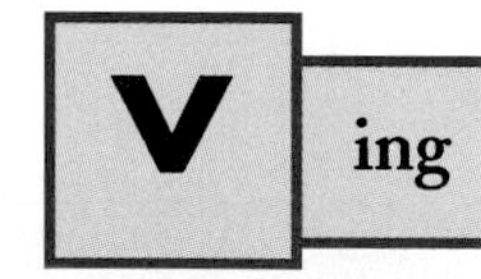

work**ing.**

They

are

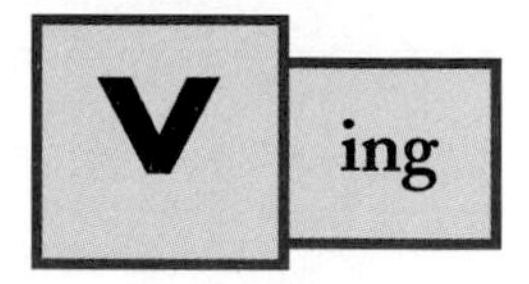

talk**ing.**

PRESENT CONTINUOUS TENSE

AFFIRMATIVE AND NEGATIVE STATEMENTS

<table>
<tr><td>I</td><td>am
'm
'm not</td><td rowspan="3">taking a break.
working on the assembly line.
loading boxes.
sleeping.
lying on the beach.
talking to the secretary.
moving boxes.</td></tr>
<tr><td>He
She
It</td><td>is
's
isn't</td></tr>
<tr><td>We
You
They</td><td>are
're
aren't</td></tr>
</table>

YES/NO QUESTIONS

<table>
<tr><td>Am</td><td>I</td><td rowspan="3">working?</td></tr>
<tr><td>Are</td><td>you
we
they</td></tr>
<tr><td>Is</td><td>he
she
it</td></tr>
</table>

•EXERCISE•

Complete these sentences about the picture on page 61. Use the present continuous tense.

1. This is the Acme Computer Company. Everyone is very busy today. Mr. Smith is in the office on the third floor. He is ________ talking ________ to the secretary.
2. Miguel is in the employee lounge. He's ____________________ a break.
3. Gina is in the warehouse. She's ____________________ boxes out to the loading platform.
4. Sam is on the loading dock. He's ____________________ boxes into the truck.
5. Joe isn't at work today. He's at home, in bed. Joe is ____________________.
6. Caroline is at home, too. She is ____________________ dinner.
7. Another worker at Acme Computer Company, Stanley Collins, is not working this week. He's on vacation. He's in Miami, Florida. He is ____________________ on the beach right now.

ON YOUR OWN

Vocabulary

Do you know these words? Find them on page 61.

- ❑ at work
- ❑ the office
- ❑ the third floor
- ❑ the second floor
- ❑ the first floor
- ❑ the employee lounge
- ❑ the factory
- ❑ the warehouse
- ❑ the loading dock
- ❑ talking to the secretary
- ❑ taking a break
- ❑ moving boxes
- ❑ loading a truck
- ❑ working on the assembly line
- ❑ on vacation
- ❑ lying on the beach
- ❑ at home
- ❑ sleeping
- ❑ cooking

Listening

Listen to your tape, and put your pictures in the correct places on your worksheet. Then check your answer on page 61.

Mr. Smith: Good morning, Ms. Brown. Is Kim at work today?

Ms. Brown: Yeah. She's working on the assembly line.

Mr. Smith: What's Gina doing right now?

Ms. Brown: She's moving boxes down in the warehouse.

Mr. Smith: Is Joe at work today?

Ms. Brown: No. He's at home. He's sick.

Mr. Smith: Where's Sam?

Ms. Brown: He's down on the loading dock. He's loading the truck.

Mr. Smith: Is Miguel helping him?

Ms. Brown: No

Mr. Smith: Why not?

Ms. Brown: Miguel is in the employee lounge. He's taking a break.

How to
tell someone you are busy

Can you help me right now?

I'm sorry. I'm busy.

CHAPTER 7

The Supermarket

Focus On

- simple present tense with **do**
- supermarket vocabulary
- polite requests

  "Could you pick up some aspirin?"
- asking about location

  "Where's the detergent?"
- telling location

  "It's in aisle 2."
- how to use **excuse me** as an apology

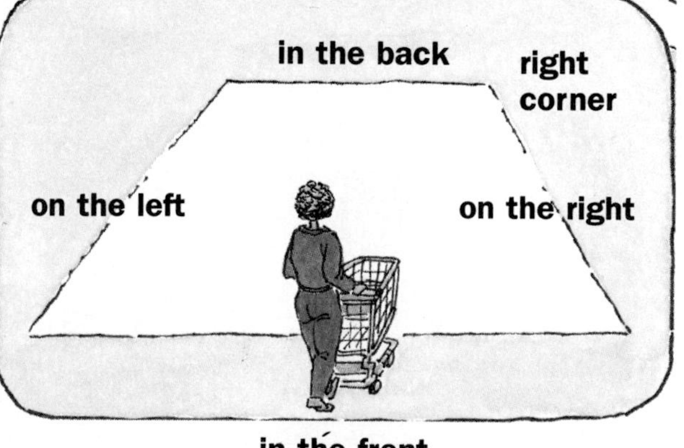

SITUATION 

Carl is shopping.

Where's	the coffee the bread the laundry detergent the aspirin the lettuce the milk the cheese	

Where are	the oranges the Band-Aids the brooms the cold cuts	

Listen

Listen and put your pictures in the correct places on your worksheet.

GROUP WORK

Practice asking and answering questions. Use your worksheet.

Reading

Read this, and put your pictures in the correct places on your worksheet.

AL'S SUPERMARKET

Al's Supermarket is big. There's a big produce section. It's in the back. They have oranges and lettuce in the produce section. The deli section is also in the back, on the right. Take-out food and cold cuts are in the deli section.

The pharmacy section is in aisle 1. They have Band-Aids and aspirin in the pharmacy section. The dairy section is in aisle 1, too. Milk and cheese are in the dairy section.

The houseware section is in aisle 2. That's where you'll find the brooms. They also have laundry detergent in the houseware section.

Writing

Write the correct words in the correct section.

PRODUCE SECTION

oranges
____

____

DAIRY SECTION

____

____

HOUSEWARE SECTION

____

____

PHARMACY SECTION

____

____

DELI SECTION

____

____

S I T U A T I O N 

Jack is looking for a broom.

Sure. They're in the back.

In the right corner.

Do you have	radios calculators cold cuts coffee aspirin	?

Listen and put your pictures in the correct places on your worksheet.

Practice asking and answering questions about an imaginary store. Ask about things the store has and doesn't have (pencils, calculators, radios, etc.). Use your worksheet.

Excuse me. Do you have aspirin?
Sure. It's in the back. On the left side.
Pardon me. Do you have calculators?
I'm sorry. We don't have calculators.

Reading

Read this, and put your pictures in the correct places on your worksheet.

SHOPPING

Jack is doing his shopping, and Sally is doing her shopping, too. Jack is in aisle 2. That's the pharmacy section. He's looking for some Band-Aids. Sally is in the produce section, on the right side of the store. She's buying oranges. She needs some laundry detergent and a broom, too. The store has laundry detergent, but it doesn't have any brooms. The detergent is in aisle 1.

Writing

Put your pictures on your worksheet. Then use your worksheet to complete these sentences.

1. The cold cuts are ______________________________.
2. The take-out food ______________________________.
3. The milk ______________________________.
4. The cheese ______________________________.
5. The coffee ______________________________.
6. The bread ______________________________.
7. The lettuce ______________________________.
8. The Band-Aids ______________________________.
9. The aspirin ______________________________.
10. The oranges ______________________________.
11. The brooms ______________________________.
12. The laundry detergent ______________________________.

Read your sentences to your group. They will put their pictures in the correct places on their worksheets.

SITUATION C

Rosa is sick. Steve is going to the store.

Could you pick up some aspirin?
Sure. Where is it in the supermarket?

Let's see . . . I think it's in the back.
OK. See you in a few minutes.

Wait! We need oranges, too. Could you get some oranges?
Where are they?

They're in the produce section, on the right.
OK. Bye.

Listen

Listen and put your pictures in the correct places on your worksheet.

GROUP WORK

Practice making requests and asking questions like these. Use your worksheet.

Could you pick up some bread?
Sure. Where are they in the supermarket?

They're ________.

Reading

Read this, and fill in the blanks below.

Every Saturday, Jack does his grocery shopping for the week. First, he gets a cart in the front of the supermarket. He goes to the deli section first. The deli section is on the right. Next he goes to the dairy section. The dairy section is in the back. The houseware section is in aisle 1. He doesn't always go to the houseware section. He only goes there if he needs something. Then he picks up the rest of his groceries. After that, he pays for his groceries. Next, he takes his food to the car. He loads it in the trunk. Then he drives home.

1. He gets a cart. ____________________

2. ____________________

3. ____________________

4. ____________________

5. ____________________

6. ____________________

Writing

Write about what you do at the market.

1. First, I get a cart.
2. Next, ____________________
3. Then, ____________________
4. ____________________
5. ____________________
6. ____________________

SITUATION 

Steve and Rosa are shopping.

CHEAP	A GOOD PRICE	EXPENSIVE
ACME BRAND COFFEE	CHOCK FULL O' BEANS COFFEE	ZAP Coffee
$1.50	$2.50	$5.00

Listen and put your pictures in the correct places on the chart above.

Ask prices for all the pictures. Then decide—is it cheap, a good price, or expensive? Put your picture in the correct column on the chart above.

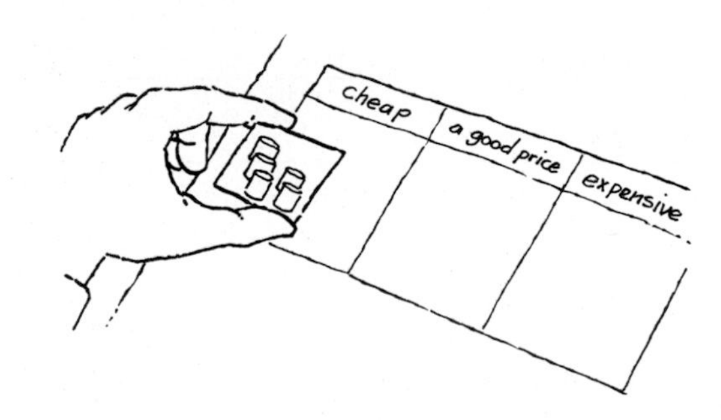

Reading

LATE FOR WORK!

Steve is at the supermarket. He's in a hurry because he's late for work. He's buying only two things, bread and coffee.

"That's really good coffee," says the clerk.

"Yes," says Steve. He is polite, but he doesn't want to talk. He's late for work.

"But it's very expensive," says the clerk.

"Yes, it is," says Steve. He looks at his watch.

"Excuse me," says a woman on the right side of the store, near the check-out stand.

"Yes?" asks the clerk.

"Where's the milk?" asks the woman.

Steve looks at his watch again. He's getting a little angry.

"It's in the dairy section in the back. On the left," says the clerk.

Writing

Continue the story. What does Steve say?

Steve says," ____

____."

The clerk says, "____

____."

____

____

____

____

GRAMMAR CHECK

A. Simple present tense with *do*

We use the base form of the verb in the simple present tense.

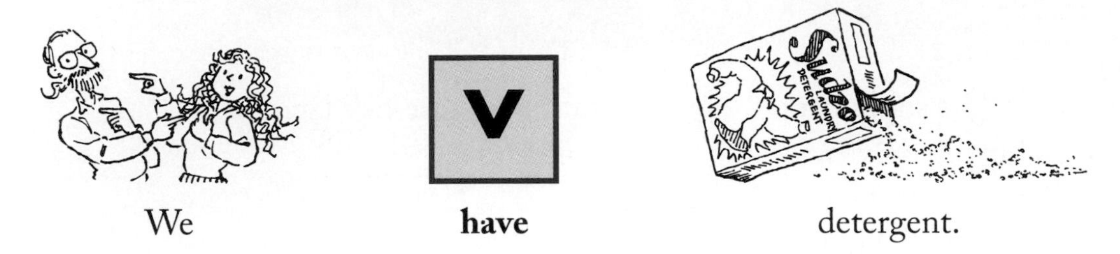

When we make questions, we put an auxiliary word (like **do**) in front of the subject.

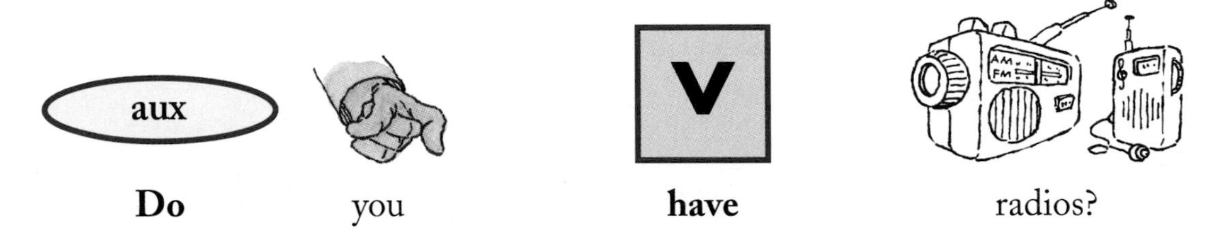

We use the auxiliary when we make a negative, too.

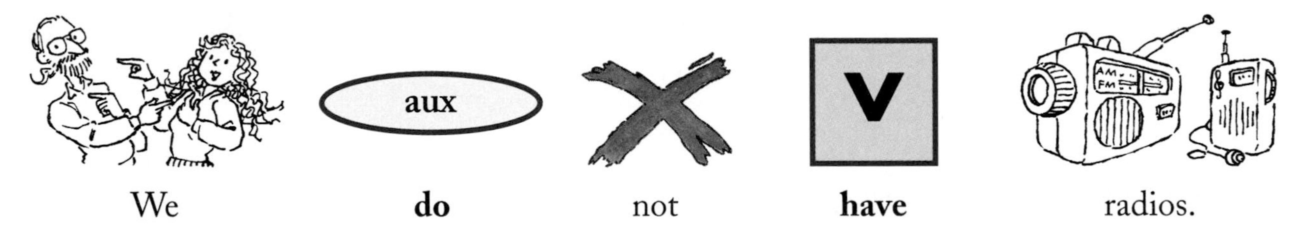

We usually make a contraction.

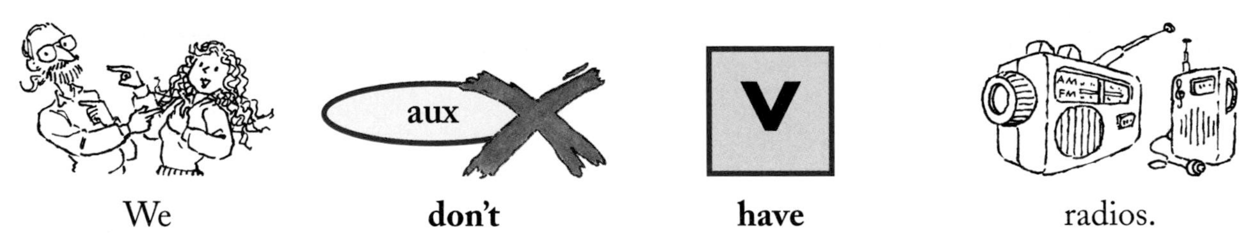

B. Review: count and noncount nouns

You can count oranges. There is a singular (an orange) and a plural (oranges) form.

You can't count laundry detergent. It is always singular in form.

SIMPLE PRESENT TENSE WITH **DO**

AFFIRMATIVE STATEMENTS

I You We They	have	brooms. oranges. take-out food. coffee.

NEGATIVE STATEMENTS

I You We They	do not don't have	brooms. oranges. take-out food. coffee.

YES/NO QUESTIONS

Do	I you we they	have	brooms oranges take-out food coffee	?

FORMAL (SHORT) ANSWERS

AFFIRMATIVE

Yes,	I we they you	do.

NEGATIVE

No,	I we they you	don't.

• EXERCISE •

Look at the picture on page 73. Complete these sentences. Use **have** or **don't have.**

1. We ___have___ take-out food.
2. We ________ coffee.
3. We ________ radios.
4. We ________ peppers.
5. They ________ lettuce.
6. They ________ TVs.
7. They ________ oranges.
8. They ________ Band-Aids.

ON YOUR OWN

Vocabulary

Do you know these words? Find them on page 73.

- ❑ coffee
- ❑ bread
- ❑ lettuce
- ❑ take-out food
- ❑ laundry detergent
- ❑ aspirin
- ❑ milk
- ❑ cheese
- ❑ oranges
- ❑ brooms
- ❑ Band-Aids
- ❑ cold cuts
- ❑ dairy section
- ❑ deli section
- ❑ produce section
- ❑ aisle
- ❑ checkout counter
- ❑ clerk
- ❑ the corner
- ❑ the top/bottom shelf
- ❑ in the front
- ❑ in the back
- ❑ on the right
- ❑ on the left

Listening

Listen to your tape and put your pictures in the correct places on your worksheet. Then check your answer on page 73.

Announcer: Jack and Sally are at the supermarket. Sally is in the back of the store behind aisle 2, near the dairy section. The deli section is also in the back of the store, on the right. Jack is in the produce section on the right side of the store. He's buying some oranges.

The clerk is in the front of the store, talking to another customer.

Customer: Pardon me. I need to buy a mop.
Clerk: I'm sorry, we don't sell mops. But we have brooms in aisle 2. They're on the bottom shelf.
Customer: O.K., thanks. While I'm here, I should also buy some milk. Do you know where that is?
Clerk: The milk is in the back of the store, in the dairy section. Do you need bread too?
Customer: Sure. Where's it at?
Clerk: The bread is on aisle 1, on the top shelf.
Customer: Thank you.
Clerk: You're welcome. Have a nice day!

How to

use *excuse me* as an apology

CHAPTER

Your Body

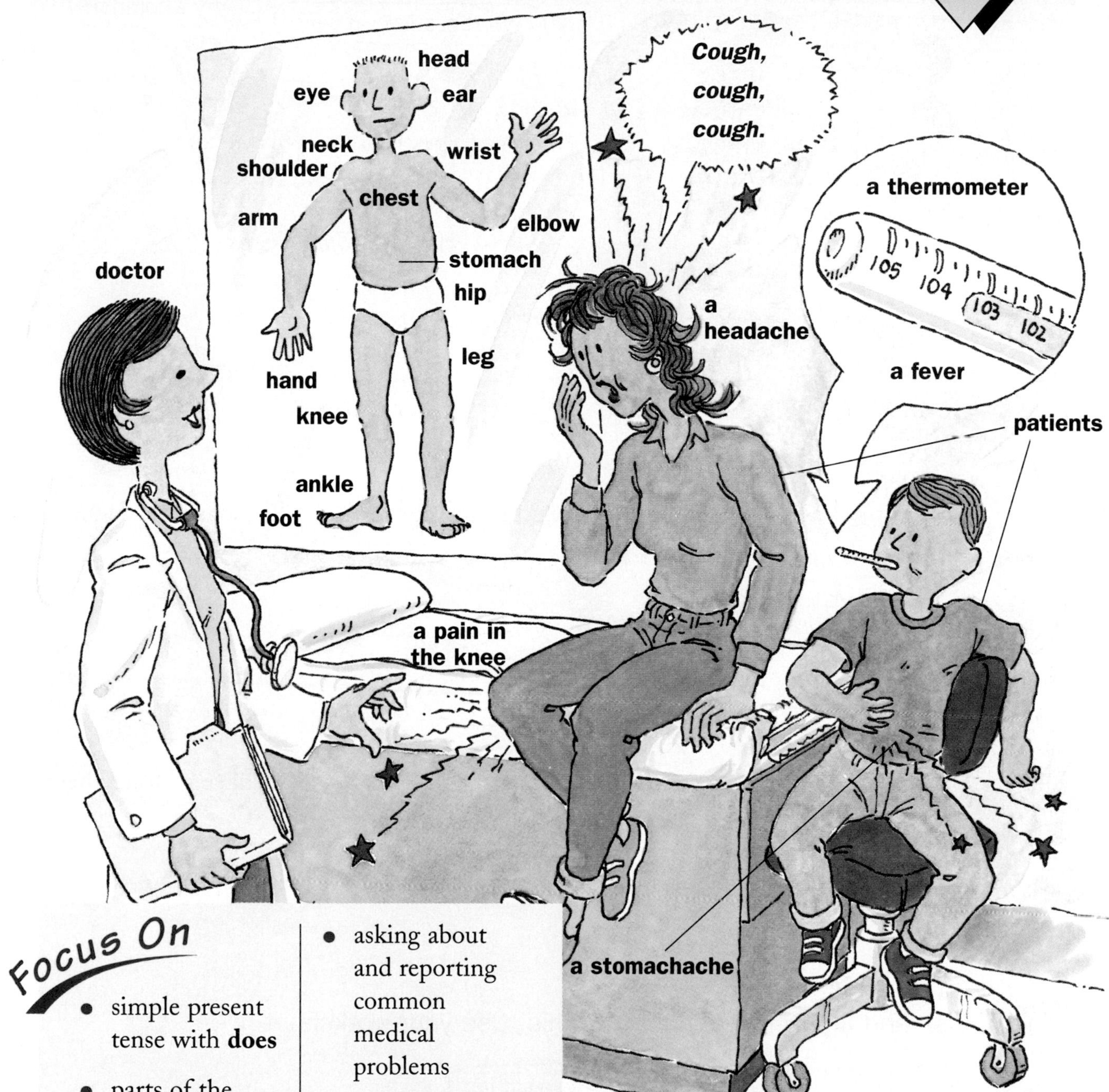

Focus On

- simple present tense with **does**
- parts of the body and medical vocabulary
- introducing yourself
  "I'm Dr. Kwon."
- asking about and reporting common medical problems
  "I have a fever."
- how to call in sick

SITUATION 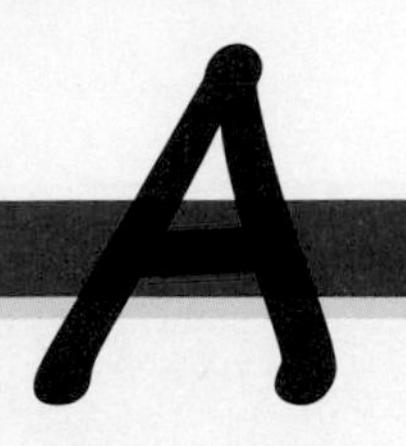
A

Nora is at the doctor's office.

Hi, I'm Dr. Kwon.
Hi, Dr. Kwon.

What's the matter?
I have a pain in my shoulder.

What's the matter?

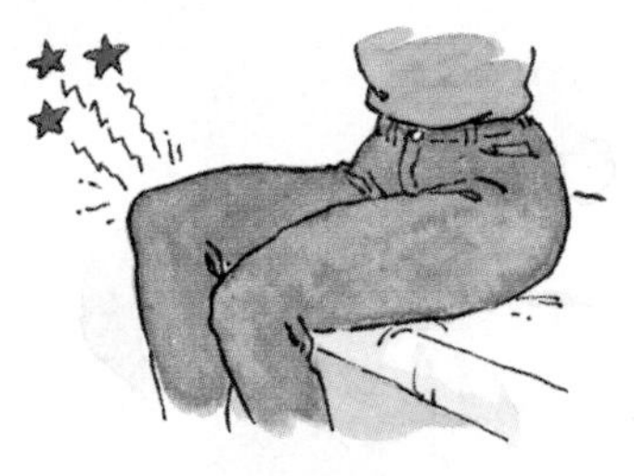

1. I have a pain in my knee.

2. I have a pain in my chest.

3. I have a headache.

cough, cough

4. I have a cough.

101
102
103

5. I have a fever.

6. I have a stomachache.

Listen

Listen and put your pictures in the correct places on your worksheet.

GROUP WORK

Ask and answer questions like this. Use your worksheet.

What's the matter?
I have a pain in my knee.

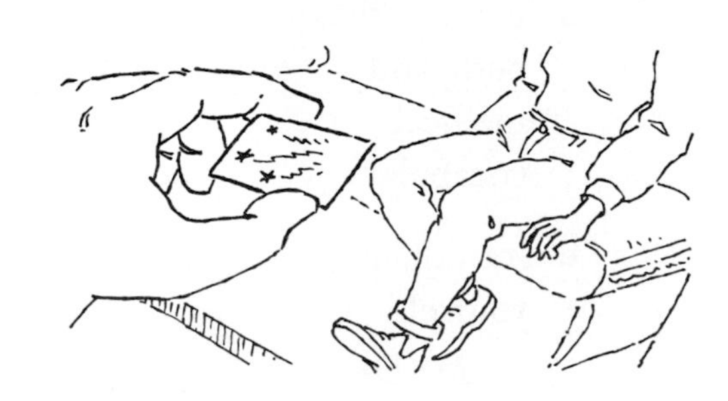

Reading

Read this, and put your pictures in the correct places on your worksheet.

NORA AND HER SON

Nora and her son Daniel are at the doctor's office. Both of them have the flu. They feel terrible. Nora has a headache and a stomachache. Daniel has a headache, but he doesn't have a stomachache. He has a fever and a pain in his chest. Nora is worried about Daniel. His fever was 104 degrees in the morning. It's only 101 degrees now, but she's still worried.

Lynn

Peter

Writing

What about Lynn and Peter? What's the matter with them?
Write about Lynn and Peter.

Peter is at the doctor's office today.

1. He has ______________________________.

2. ______________________________.

3. ______________________________.

Lynn is at the doctor's office, too.

4. She has ______________________________.

5. ______________________________.

6. ______________________________.

7. ______________________________.

Read your sentences to the class. They will put their pictures in the correct places on their worksheets.

SITUATION B

Donald is at the doctor's office with his son and daughter.

Good morning.
I'm Dr. Martinez.
Hi, Dr. Martinez.
Both your son and your daughter are here today, huh? What's the matter with them?
They both have bad stomachaches.
Stomachaches, huh? Do they have any other symptoms?
My son doesn't. But my daughter has a headache, too.
Hmmmmm. Does she have a fever?
No.

Listen *Listen and put your pictures in the correct places on your worksheet.*

GROUP WORK Role-play a doctor and a parent with one small child. Use your worksheet.

Good evening.
I'm Dr. Martinez.
Hi, Dr. Martinez.
What's the matter with you?
I have a ____, and my son has a ____.

Reading/Writing

Read this, and then continue the story below.

DONALD'S PROBLEMS

Donald was sick yesterday. He didn't go to work. He went to the doctor's office.

"What's the matter?" the doctor asked.

"I feel terrible," said Donald. "I have a headache and a fever."

"Do you have any other symptoms?" asked the doctor.

"No, just the headache and fever," said Donald.

What did Donald say? What did the doctor say? Write the words that Donald said and the words that the doctor said.

S I T U A T I O N

Dr. Kwon and Dr. Martinez give advice.

For a cough . . .

For a fever, a headache, or body pains . . .

For a stomachache . . .

For body pains or muscle aches . . .

Listen and put your pictures in the correct places on your worksheet.

GROUP WORK

Role-play a doctor and a patient. Give advice.

Reading 

Read this, and put your pictures in the correct places on your worksheet.

NORA'S PROBLEM

Nora was sick yesterday. She had a fever and a headache. She also had pains in her arms and legs. She felt terrible. She called her doctor.

"Take two aspirin," the doctor said. "And stay home."

Nora called her boss at work.

"I'm sick, Mr. Smith," Nora said. "I have a fever and a headache."

"I'm sorry to hear that," Mr. Smith said. "I hope you feel better soon."

Writing 

Nora called her mother. What did Nora say? What did her mother say? Continue their conversation by writing in the blank spaces below.

SITUATION 

Antonio and Mario are talking about a new student.

Listen and put your pictures in the correct places on your worksheet.

GROUP WORK

Practice asking and answering questions about an imaginary family. Use all of your pictures.

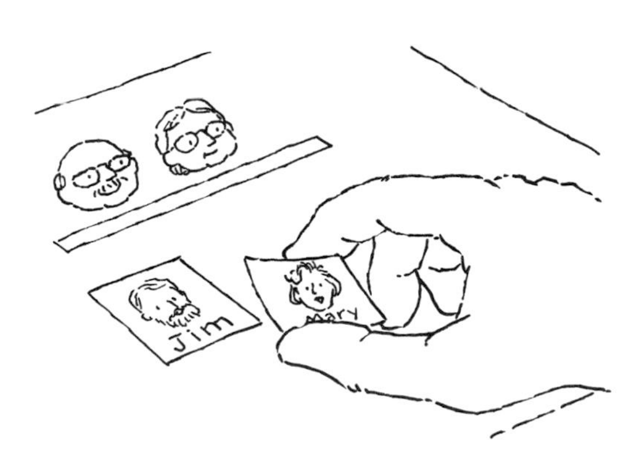

Reading

Read this, and answer the questions below.

MIKE'S FAMILY

Mike is from New York, but he lives in Chicago now. He is from a large family. He has two brothers and three sisters. His brother, Mark, lives in Chicago, too. Mike is single, but Mark is married. His wife's name is Paula. They got married last year. They don't have any children.

Mike's mother lives in New York. His father is dead. Mike's three sisters, Michele, Maggie, and Mary Liz, all live in New York, too. His other brother, Monty, lives in Los Angeles. He's divorced.

Who lives in Chicago?	Who lives in New York?	Who lives in Los Angeles?
______________	______________	______________
______________	______________	
______________	______________	
	______________	

Writing

Write about your family.

1. I'm from ______________________.
2. I live in ______________________ now.
3. I have ______________ brothers and ______________ sisters.
4. ______________________.
5. ______________________.

Extra *Draw a picture of your family tree.*

SITUATION D

Bob Lee is showing Gloria photos of his family.

Who's that?
That's my brother.
Where does he live?
He lives in Taiwan.
This is my sister.
Does she live in Taiwan, too?
No. She lives here.

Where do Antonio's brother and sisters live? Listen and put your pictures in the correct places below.

HERE	ANOTHER COUNTRY

Use your pictures. Talk about your family. Where are your brothers and sisters? Use your pictures and the chart above.

I have two brothers. One brother is in Haiti. One brother is here.

Reading

Read this, and use your pictures to make a family tree.

My name is Jim Butler. I'm married. My wife's name is Ellen. We have one child, a boy. His name is Tom. I have one brother. His name is Ron. He lives in Miami. Ron is married. His wife's name is Mary. They have three children. Their names are Kathy, Beth, and April. I have one sister. Her name is Amy. She's single. She lives in Seattle.

Writing

Write about your family.

My name is ______________________. ______________________

____

____

____

____

____

____

____

____

____

____

GRAMMAR CHECK

A. Possessive Adjectives

Hi. I'm Ron.
That's my wife.

my wife

our children

his wife

their children

her husband

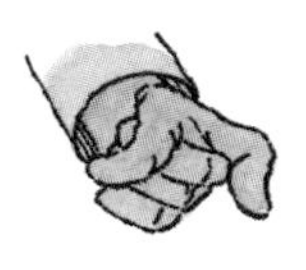

your

children

B. Possessive Using 's

Amy

Be

is

Ron**'s**

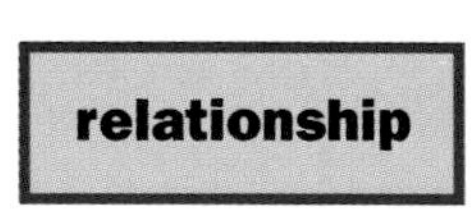
relationship

wife.

Look at the difference.

Be

Amy**'s**

relationship

Ron**'s**

wife.

Amy**'s** = Amy **is**

Ron**'s** = **of** Ron (possessive)

POSSESSIVE ADJECTIVES

<table>
<tr><td>Ron</td><td rowspan="2">is</td><td rowspan="2">my
his
her
your
our
their</td><td>brother-in-law.
son.
husband.
father.
brother.
uncle.</td></tr>
<tr><td>Susan</td><td>wife.
mother.
sister.
aunt.
daughter.
sister-in-law.</td></tr>
</table>

POSSESSIVE WITH 'S

<table>
<tr><td>Ron</td><td rowspan="2">is</td><td rowspan="2">Susan
April
Ron
Ellen
Tom</td><td rowspan="2">'s</td><td>brother-in-law.
son.
husband.
father.
brother.</td></tr>
<tr><td>Susan</td><td>wife.
mother.
sister.
daughter.
sister-in-law.</td></tr>
</table>

QUESTIONS WITH **HAVE**

<table>
<tr><td>Do</td><td>you
they</td><td rowspan="2">have</td><td rowspan="2">any children
any brothers
any sisters</td><td rowspan="2">?</td></tr>
<tr><td>Does</td><td>he
she</td></tr>
</table>

QUESTIONS WITH **BE**

<table>
<tr><td>Are</td><td>you
they</td><td rowspan="2">married
single</td><td rowspan="2">?</td></tr>
<tr><td>Is</td><td>he
she</td></tr>
</table>

• EXERCISE •

Look at the picture on page 97. Then complete the sentences below.

1. Ron is ___Frank's___ brother.

2. Amy is ______________ wife.

3. Ron is ______________ husband.

4. Tom is ______________ son.

5. Ron is ______________ father.

6. April is ______________ daughter.

7. Ron is ______________ father.

8. Susan is ______________ sister-in-law.

9. Ron is ______________ brother-in-law.

ON YOUR OWN

Vocabulary

Do you know these words? Find them on page 97.

❑ sister-in-law ❑ wife ❑ daughter ❑ uncle
❑ brother ❑ husband ❑ mother ❑ grandfather
❑ nephew ❑ father ❑ aunt ❑ grandmother
❑ niece ❑ son ❑ cousins ❑ sister

Listening

Listen to your tape and put your pictures in the correct places on your worksheet. Then check your answer on page 97.

Ron: Hi. My name is Ron. I'm married. My wife's name is Amy. We have two kids, a son and a daughter. My son's name is Tom and my daughter's name is April. They're great kids! My brother Frank has two kids, too. He has a son and a daughter. My nephew's name is Alan and my niece's name is Beth.

Tom: I'm Tom. My father's name is Ron. Of course, I call him Dad. My mom's name is Amy. I have two cousins, Alan and Beth. I really like my aunt and uncle. My aunt's name is Susan. My uncle's name is Frank.

How to
introduce yourself

In formal situations we usually shake hands.

In informal situations we don't usually shake hands.

A Daily Schedule

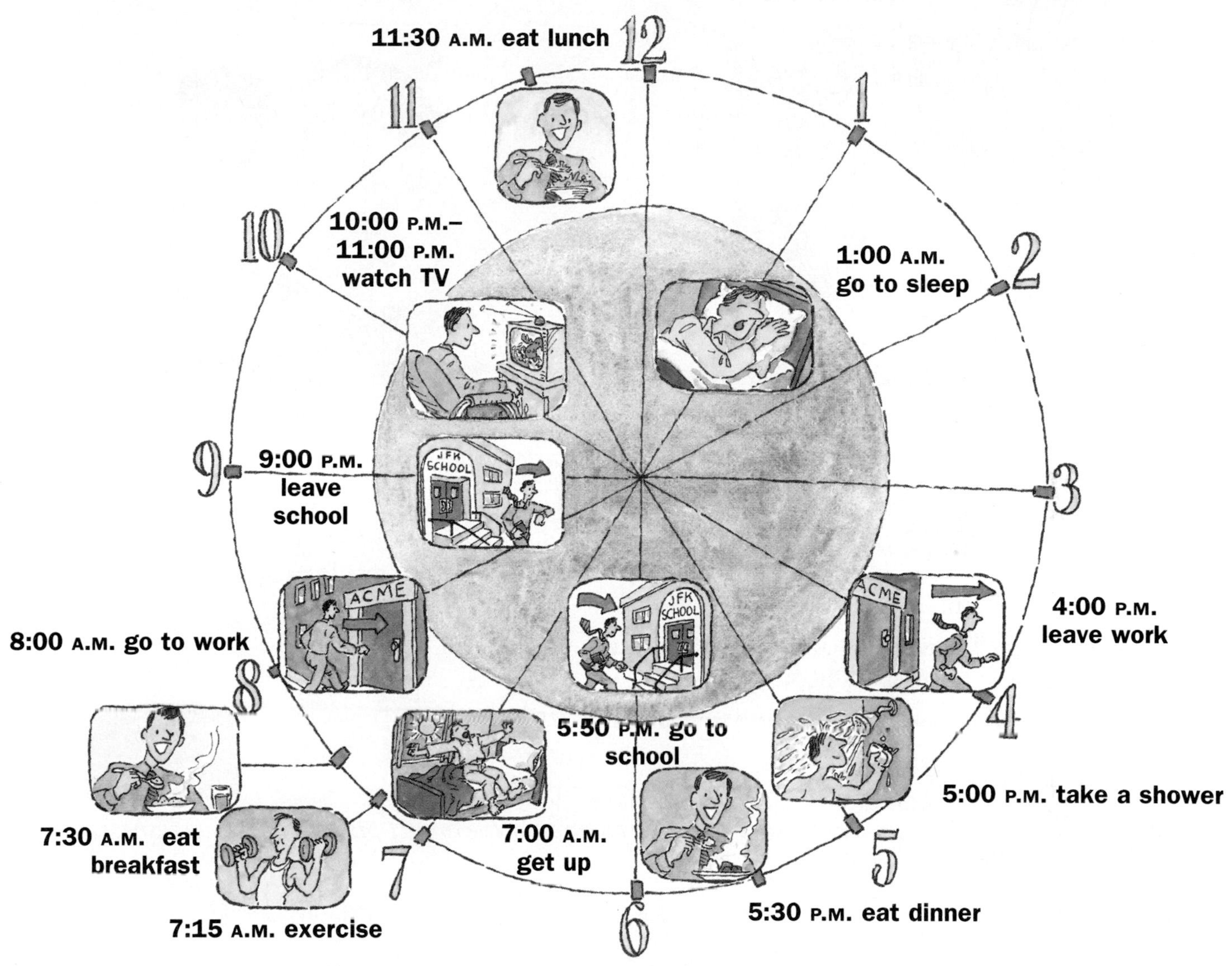

Focus On

- simple present tense
- frequency adverbs
- vocabulary for daily activities
- describing a typical schedule
  "I get up at 7 A.M."
- how to ask for more information when an answer is negative

SITUATION 

Margie and Matt are talking.

Listen and put your pictures in the correct places on your worksheet.

Practice asking these questions. Use your worksheet.

Reading

Read this, and answer the questions below.

RAY'S SCHEDULE

Ray has a hard schedule. His work hours change all the time. He usually goes to work at 8:00 in the morning. But sometimes he works the night shift. Then he goes to work at 5:00 in the afternoon.

Ray usually goes to sleep around 11:00 at night, but sometimes he goes to sleep at 4:00 in the morning. It's hard to change your schedule. Sometimes Ray is very tired because he doesn't get enough sleep.

usually = 80–90% of the time (four days a week; 22–28 days a month)

1. Ray usually goes to work at ___________.
2. Ray usually goes to sleep at ___________.

sometimes = 30–50% of the time (one day a week; 8–16 days a month)

1. Sometimes Ray goes to work at ________.
2. Sometimes Ray goes to sleep at ________.

Writing

Write about your schedule.

1. I usually get up at ____.
2. I usually go to bed at ____.
3. I usually get ______________________________________ hours of sleep.

Write about a classmate's schedule.

1. ______________________ usually gets up at ______________________.
2. ______________________ usually goes to bed at ___________________.
3. ______________________ usually gets ________________ hours of sleep.

SITUATION B

Lee is asking Anita about her schedule.

Do you	work? go to school? eat breakfast?

What time do you	go to work? leave work? eat breakfast? go to school? leave school?

Listen and put your pictures in the correct places on your worksheet.

GROUP WORK

Practice asking and answering questions like these. Use your worksheet.

Reading

Read this, and put your pictures in the correct places on your worksheet.

ANITA'S SCHEDULE

Anita has a very busy schedule. She works five days a week from 8:30 A.M. to 4:30 P.M. She gets up at 6:30 A.M. every day to get ready for work. She takes a shower and eats breakfast, then goes to work at around 7:30 A.M.

Anita's lunch break is at noon. At 4:30, she leaves work and goes home. At home, she eats dinner, usually around 5:00 P.M. Sometimes she exercises after dinner.

She goes to school at 6:30. School is over at 9:00 P.M., and she goes home again. Anita usually watches TV from 10 to 11 P.M. Then she goes to sleep because she has to get up the next morning at 6:30.

Writing

Write about your schedule.

1. I get up at ______________________________.
2. I eat breakfast at ______________________________.
3. ______________________________.
4. ______________________________.
5. ______________________________.
6. ______________________________.
7. ______________________________.

Extra *Read your sentences to the class. They will put their pictures in the correct places on their worksheets.*

S I T U A T I O N

Dave Collins won seven million dollars in the lottery.

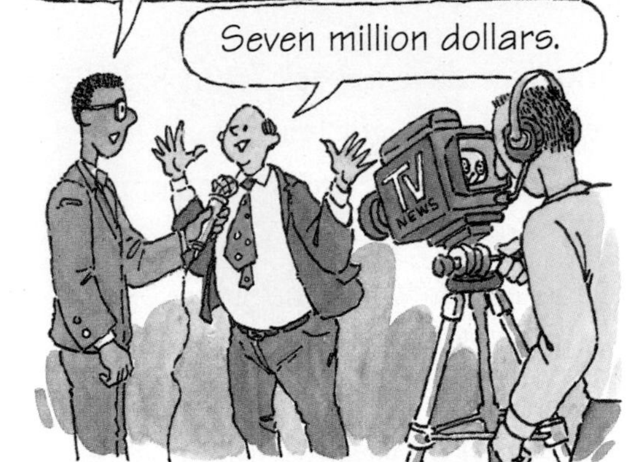

Listen

Listen and put your pictures in the correct places on your worksheet.

GROUP WORK

Imagine you won the lottery. Then tell the group about your schedule. Use your worksheet.

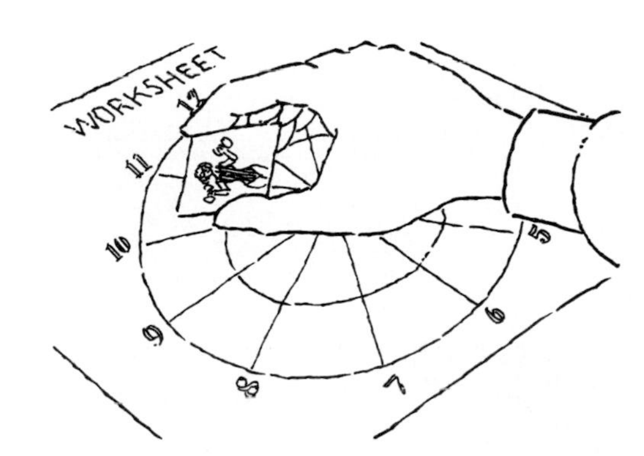

Reading

Read this, and put your pictures in the correct places on your worksheet.

The Richest Woman in America

Mrs. Abigail Van Johnson is the richest woman in America. Her daily schedule is very different from most other people's daily schedules. For one thing, she doesn't work. She gets up at 7:00 A.M. every morning, but she doesn't have to get ready for work. Instead, she relaxes. She reads the paper and drinks coffee for two hours. Then, around 9:00, she goes downstairs and eats her breakfast. After breakfast, at 10:00, she exercises for an hour. After she's done exercising, she's hungry again, so she eats lunch.

Writing

Continue the story. What does Mrs. Van Johnson do after lunch?

She eats lunch from ____________ to ____________. After lunch,

she ____

______________________________________. Then, in the afternoon, she

____.

At night, she ______________________________________

____

____

____.

SITUATION D

Lee is talking about his morning schedule.

First I get up at exactly 7:00 A.M.

Then, I take a shower.

After that, I eat breakfast around 7:30.

I watch TV for a while, maybe fifteen minutes.

Then I exercise for around twenty minutes.

After that, I go to work. I usually get to work by 8:30.

Listen and put your pictures in the correct places on your worksheet.

GROUP WORK

Talk about your morning schedule. What do you do first? After that?

Words to use
- exactly
- first
- next
- around
- after that
- for a while

Reading

Read this and fill in the lists. What does Charlie do? What doesn't he do?

CHARLIE NEVER HAS TIME!

I'm always late in the morning. I never have enough time. I get up at 6:00, and I have a cup of coffee. I don't eat breakfast because I don't have time. I'd like to watch TV but I can't because I'm always late. I take a shower, but I don't exercise. I need to exercise, but I don't do it because I just don't have time.

My wife says, "You never talk to me in the morning!"

It's true. I don't talk to her. I don't have time!

Things Charlie does	Things Charlie doesn't do
______________________	______________________
______________________	______________________
______________________	______________________
______________________	______________________
______________________	______________________

Writing

Write about your morning schedule.

I get up at __________. First, I ____

______________________________. Next I ______________________________

__________. After that I ____

____

____

____.

A. Simple present tense

We use the simple present tense when we talk about things we do every day.
For **I**, **we**, **you**, or **they**, use the simple form of the verb.

Put an **s** (or **es**) when you use third person singular (one man, one woman, one thing).

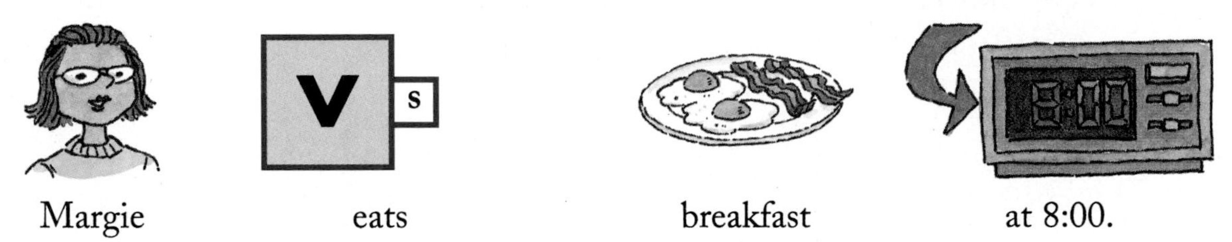

Move **es** to the auxiliary in the third person singular when you make questions.

B. Frequency adverbs

These words answer the question "How often?" Notice how the position with **be** is different from other verbs.

SIMPLE PRESENT TENSE

I You We They	get up	at 8:30. at 9:00. around 8:00.
He She	gets up	

QUESTIONS IN SIMPLE PRESENT

What time	do	I we they you	go to work get up go to bed	?
	does	he she		

FREQUENCY ADVERBS

I You We They	always usually never sometimes	eat breakfast.
He She		eats breakfast.

I	am	always usually Sometimes never	tired. late.
He She	is		
You We They	are		

• EXERCISE •

Look at the picture on page 109. Then complete these sentences. Remember to use **s** or **es** with third person singular (one man, one woman, one thing).

1. At 7:00 A.M., Matt ____________________.
2. At 7:30 in the morning, he ____________________.
3. At 8:00 in the morning, he ____________________.
4. He always ____________________ at 4 P.M.
5. At 5:30 P.M., he ____________________.
6. He ____________________ at 5:50 P.M.
7. He ____________________ at 9 P.M.
8. From 10:00 to 11:00 P.M., he ____________________.
9. At 1 A.M., he ____________________.

ON YOUR OWN

Vocabulary

Do you know these words? Find them on page 109.

❑ a daily schedule	❑ go to school	❑ eat dinner	❑ go to sleep
❑ get up	❑ leave work	❑ eat lunch	❑ go to work
❑ exercise	❑ take a shower	❑ watch TV	❑ leave school

Listening

Listen to your tape, and put your pictures in the correct places on your worksheet. Then check your answer on page 109.

Margie: You look tired!

Matt: I am. I get up at 7 A.M. every morning.

Margie: That's not so early. What time do you go to bed?

Matt: Usually about one o'clock in the morning.

Margie: Oh, that's why you're tired. You only get six hours of sleep! Do you exercise?

Matt: Yeah, I usually exercise first thing in the morning after I get up at around 7:15. Then I eat breakfast at around 7:30.

Margie: And what time do you go to work?

Matt: At around 8 A.M.

Margie: You go to school after work, don't you?

Matt: Yeah. My class starts at 6:30 P.M., so I usually go to school at around 6.

Margie: You don't have much free time. No wonder you're so tired!

How to

ask for more information when an answer is negative

How was your weekend?
Not very good.
That's too bad. Why?
I didn't do anything. I stayed home all weekend.

Verb Charts

base form	*past form*	*continuous*	*meaning in your language*
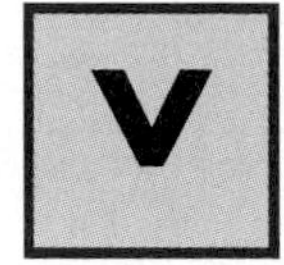	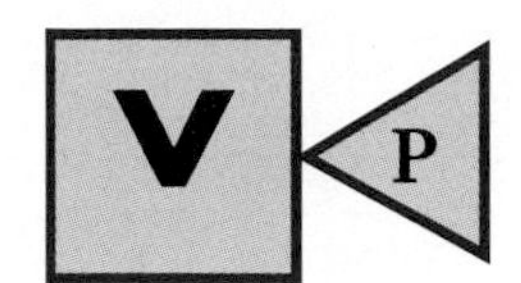	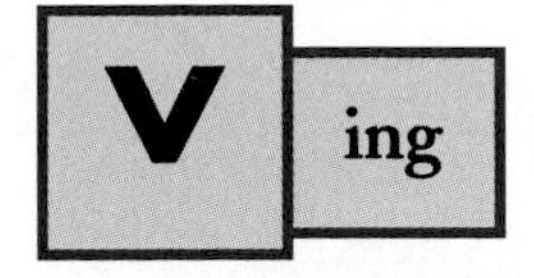	
be (am/is/are)	was/were	being	
act	acted	acting	
address	addressed	addressing	
answer	answered	answering	
apologize	apologized	apologizing	
appear	appeared	appearing	
arrive	arrived	arriving	
ask	asked	asking	
assemble	assembled	assembling	
begin	began/begun	beginning	
break	broke	breaking	
buy	bought	buying	
call	called	calling	

base form	*past form*	*continuous*	*meaning in your language*
V	V ◁ P	V ing	
change	changed	changing	
check	checked	checking	
choose	chose	choosing	
circle	circled	circling	
clarify	clarified	clarifying	
clean	cleaned	cleaning	
close	closed	closing	
come	came	coming	
complete	completed	completing	
continue	continued	continuing	
cook	cooked	cooking	
count	counted	counting	
cover	covered	covering	
cut	cut	cutting	
decide	decided	deciding	
describe	described	describing	

base form	past form	continuous	meaning in your language
V	V P	V ing	
die	died	dying	
divorce	divorced	divorcing	
do	did	doing	
draw	drew	drawing	
drink	drank/drunk	drinking	
drive	drove	driving	
eat	ate	eating	
excuse	excused	excusing	
exercise	exercised	exercising	
feel	felt	feeling	
fill	filled	filling	
fill in	filled in	filling in	
find	found	finding	
follow	followed	following	
form	formed	forming	
get	got	getting	

base form	*past form*	*continuous*	*meaning in your language*
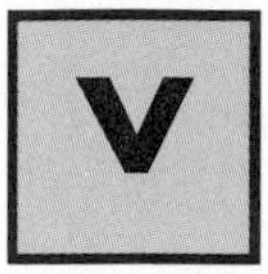 V	 V + P	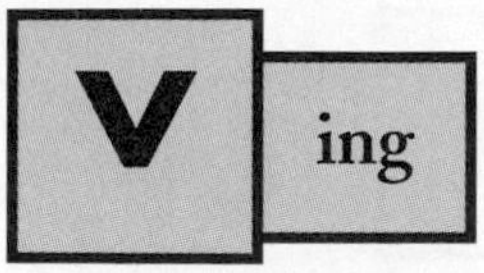 V + ing	
get up	got up	getting up	
give	gave	giving	
go	went	going	
guess	guessed	guessing	
happen	happened	happening	
have	had	having	
hear	heard	hearing	
help	helped	helping	
hope	hoped	hoping	
imagine	imagined	imagining	
introduce	introduced	introducing	
know	knew	knowing	
leave	left	leaving	
let	let	letting	
lie	lay	lying	
like	liked	liking	

base form	past form	continuous	meaning in your language
V	V P	V ing	
listen	listened	listening	
live	lived	living	
load	loaded	loading	
look	looked	looking	
love	loved	loving	
make	made	making	
marry	married	marrying	
match	matched	matching	
meet	met	meeting	
miss	missed	missing	
move	moved	moving	
need	needed	needing	
order	ordered	ordering	
pardon	pardoned	pardoning	
pay	paid	paying	
pick up	picked up	picking up	

base form	past form	continuous	meaning in your language
 V	 V P	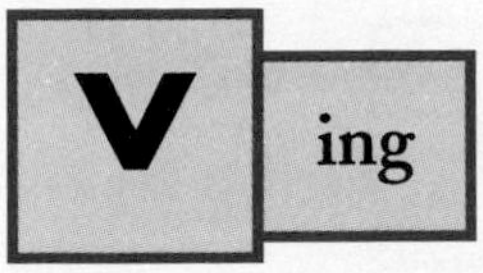 V ing	
play	played	playing	
practice	practiced	practicing	
put	put	putting	
read	read	reading	
register	registered	registering	
relax	relaxed	relaxing	
remember	remembered	remembering	
repeat	repeated	repeating	
report	reported	reporting	
request	requested	requesting	
rub	rubbed	rubbing	
say	said	saying	
see	saw	seeing	
sell	sold	selling	
share	shared	sharing	
shop	shopped	shopping	

base form	*past form*	*continuous*	*meaning in your language*
V	V P	V ing	
show	showed	showing	
sit	sat	sitting	
sleep	slept	sleeping	
speak	spoke	speaking	
start	started	starting	
stay	stayed	staying	
stir	stirred	stirring	
study	studied	studying	
take	took	taking	
talk	talked	talking	
teach	taught	teaching	
tell	told	telling	
thank	thanked	thanking	
think	thought	thinking	
turn	turned	turning	
use	used	using	

base form	*past form*	*continuous*	*meaning in your language*
	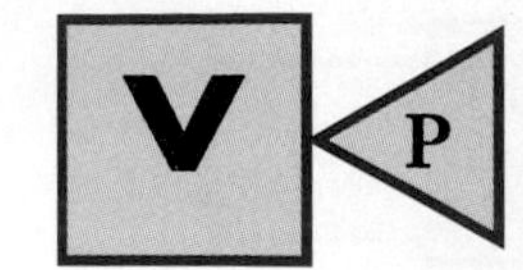	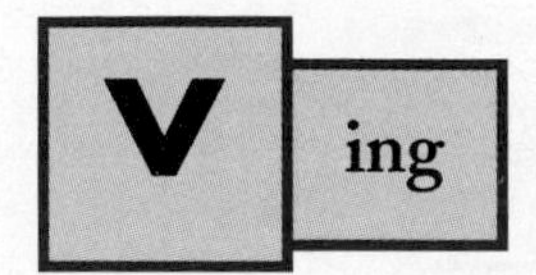	
visit	visited	visiting	
want	wanted	wanting	
watch	watched	watching	
win	won	winning	
work	worked	working	
worry	worried	worrying	
write	wrote	writing	

Dialogues

CHAPTER 1
School

Situation A, page 2

Narrator: This is the office of an adult school. The secretary is busy helping some students register for English class.

A: OK. Here's your registration. You're in room 2. Room 2 is next to the bookstore.
B: Thank you.

A: Here's your registration. You're in room 3. Room 3 is next to the cafeteria.
B: Thank you.

A: Here you go. You're in room 7. That's right across from room 2.
B: Thanks.

A: Excuse me, where is the (women's/men's) room?
B: The (women's/men's) room? It's just down the hall, next to room 7. Across from the bookstore.
A: Thanks.

Situation B, page 4

Narrator: It's a busy day at school. Many students are in the hall asking for directions.

A: Excuse me, where's room 13?
B: It's next to the bookstore.
A: Thanks.

A: Excuse me, where's the (women's/men's) room?
B: Let's see . . . it's . . . uh . . . next to the cafeteria. Across from the office.
A: Next to the cafeteria?
B: Yeah.
A: Thanks a lot.

A: (*speak softly*) Excuse me, where is room 56?
B: I'm sorry. Could you repeat that?
A: Sure. Where is room 56?
B: Oh, 56? It's across from the cafeteria. Next to the office.
A: Thanks.
B: Sure.

Situation C, page 6

Narrator: At the school, these students are looking for their teachers.

A: Excuse me, where's Mr. Sanchez?
B: He's in room 14.
A: Where's room 14?
B: It's across from the cafeteria.
A: Thanks.

A: Excuse me, where's Ms. Williams?
B: Ms. Williams is in . . . let's see here . . . here it is, room 37.
A: Where is room 37?
B: It's next to the bookstore. At the end of the hall.
A: Thank you.

Situation D, page 8

Narrator: Look at the map. You are at the front door. Listen and follow the directions with your finger.

A: OK, let's see now . . . go straight, turn left, then go straight and turn right, then turn left and . . . the room is there.
And that's room . . . uh . . . one?
A: Uh-huh.

Narrator: Try again. Remember to start at the front door.

A: OK. Go straight and turn right . . . then turn left . . . and turn left again. That's your room.
B: That's room 3, right?
A: Yes.

CHAPTER 2
A Kitchen

Situation A, page 14

Narrator: These people are putting away their groceries.

A: *(name)*, could you put the tomatoes on the counter?
B: Sure.
A: Thanks.

A: Oh, *(name)*, could you put the onions in the cabinet for me?
B: Sure.
A: Thank you.

A: *(name)*, could you put the egg in the refrigerator?
B: The egg?
A: Yeah, the single one, over there. I don't need it.
B: OK.
A: Thanks.

Situation B, page 16

Narrator: These friends are cooking together in the kitchen.

A: *(name)*, where's the bowl?
B: It's on the shelf over there.
A: Oh, yeah, I got it.
A: *(name)*, where are the peppers? I can't find them anywhere.
B: They're in the refrigerator. I put them there.
A: Oh, yeah, that's right.

A: *(speak softly)* *(name)*, where are the tomatoes?
B: The what?
A: The tomatoes.
B: Oh, they're on the counter over there.
A: Oh, yeah, I see them.

Situation C, page 18

Narrator: It's time for dinner. These friends are cooking in the kitchen.

A: Is the spoon in the drawer?
B: Uh-uh. It's on the shelf.

A: Are the tomatoes in the refrigerator?
B: Uh-huh.
A: Oh, yeah, I see them.

A: Are the onions in the refrigerator?
B: Uh . . . I'm not sure.
A: No. They're not here.
B: Try the cabinet.
A: Oh, yeah. Here they are.

Situation D, page 20

Narrator: In the kitchen, these friends are busy cooking breakfast. Listen and circle the words that you hear.

A: What are you making?
B: Scrambled eggs.
A: Can I help?
B: Sure, thanks. I need six eggs.
A: Are they in the refrigerator?
B: Yeah.
A: OK. Do you need anything else from the refrigerator?
B: Uh, let's see . . . a pepper, and uh . . . an onion. They're all in the refrigerator on the bottom shelf.
A: OK. I got them. Do you need anything else?
B: A knife and a frying pan. The knife is in the drawer next to the refrigerator and the frying pan is on the stove.
A: OK. I got everything.

CHAPTER 3

Time

Situation A, page 26

Narrator: **These people are all on their way to work. What time is it?**

A: Excuse me, what time is it?
B: It's . . . uh . . . 11:00.
A: Thanks.

Narrator: **Clear your worksheet and listen again.**

A: What time is it?
B: It's 3:30.
A: 3:30?
B: That's right.

Narrator: **Clear your worksheet and listen again.**

A: Excuse me, what time is it right now?
B: Right now? Uh . . . exactly 4:52.
A: Thanks.

Narrator: **Clear your worksheet and listen again.**

A: Hey, *(name)*. What time is it?
B: I'm not sure. I think it's around 9:45.

Situation B, page 28

Narrator: **You answer the phone. Your (husband's/wife's) friend is calling.**

A: Hello?
B: Hi, this is *(name)*. Is *(name)* there?
A: Oh, hi *(name)*. No, (he's/she's) not here. What time is it?
B: Uh . . . about 8:20.
A: Oh, (he's/she's) probably still on his way to work.
B: Oh, OK. I'll call (him/her) at work later. Thanks.
A: OK. Take care.
B: Bye.

Narrator: **Clear your worksheet. Your phone rings again. It's your (wife/husband).**

A: Hello?
B: Hi, honey.
A: Hi, *(name)*. Where are you? It's almost seven o'clock.
B: Yeah, I know. I'm at work still. I'm leaving right now.
A: Oh, OK. See you in a while then.
B: Yeah. See you in about 20 minutes.
A: OK. Bye.

Situation C, page 30

Narrator: **On the street, a reporter is asking people questions.**

A: Hi!
B: Hello.
A: I'm *(name)* of WBBS Radio. I'd like to ask you a question.
B: OK.
A: Where are you usually at 9:30 a.m.?
B: I'm at work.
A: Do you listen to WBBS?
B: Yes, every day.
A: Congratulations. Here's a free coffee mug.

A: Excuse me, (Sir/Ma'am)?
B: Yes?
A: *(name)*, WBBS Radio. Where are you usually at 9:30?
B: A.M.?
A: Yes.
B: I'm at school.
A: Do you listen to WBBS?
B: At school? No.
A: Well, here's a free coffee mug anyway.

Situation D, page 32

Narrator: **These friends run into each other on the street near the adult school.**

A: Hi *(name)*!
B: Oh, hi *(name)*. How are you?
A: Fine. What's new?
B: Not much. What time is it, *(name)*?
A: It's uh . . . five fifty-five.
B: Oh, gosh, I'm really late for my class.
A: What time does your class start?
B: Six o'clock. I'm on my way right now. Sorry, I have to run. See you later.
A: OK. So long.

CHAPTER 4

A Restaurant

Situation A, page 38

Narrator: This catering truck has good food. Many people are ordering something to eat.

A: Hello. Can I help you?
B: Uh . . . how much is a soda?
A: Sixty cents.

A: Morning.
B: Good morning. Can I help you?
A: How much is a bowl of soup?
B: It's one-fifty.

A: Excuse me.
B: Oh, hi. Can I help you?
A: How much is a slice of pie?
B: A buck twenty-five.
A: One twenty-five?
B: That's right.

Situation B, page 40

Narrator: Lots of people come to eat at this popular restaurant.

A: Good afternoon. Are you ready to order?
B: Yes. I'd like a bowl of soup, please.
A: OK. Anything else?
B: Let's see . . . a cup of coffee also.
A: OK. Is that all? Can I get you a salad?
B: Uh . . . OK, a salad sounds good.

A: Good evening. Are you ready to order?
B: Yes, I'd like a hot dog, please.
A: Anything else? Something to drink?
B: A Coke.
A: Is Pepsi OK?
B: Yeah, fine.
A: OK. Just a few minutes.

Situation C, page 42

Narrator: These people want to know how much food costs in other countries.

A: Where are you from?
B: I'm from Tokyo.
A: Tokyo's expensive, isn't it?
B: Yes. The prices are very high. A soda is . . . let's see . . . almost a buck-fifty. And an order of french fries at McDonald's is . . . about a dollar eighty.
A: Wow! That's really expensive!

A: Where are you from?
B: Midlands, Texas. It's a pretty small place.
A: Is everything cheaper there?
B: Oh, yes. Especially food. This city is very expensive. In Midlands, a cup of coffee is forty-five cents. Here, sometimes it's a dollar. And a hamburger is seventy-five cents at the place in Midlands. Here, it's two dollars or more!

Situation D, page 44

Narrator: It's another busy day at everyone's favorite restaurant.

A: Good afternoon. Would you like a menu?
B: I don't know . . . what's good?
A: Well, the salad is great. It's a good deal.
B: How much is it?
A: It's only one twenty-five.
B: OK. That sounds good.

A: Good evening. Can I get you a menu?
B: I'm in a hurry. What's good?
A: The chicken sandwiches are very good. We make them with real roast chicken.
B: How much is a sandwich?
A: It's only one-fifty.
B: Hmm. That sounds good. OK, give me a chicken sandwich.

CHAPTER 5 Your Neighborhood

Situation A, page 50

Narrator: **These people are going to see each other tomorrow. They are describing where they live.**

A: I'll come by your place.
B: OK. Great.
A: Where do you live?
B: 1435 Washington Avenue. It's a big apartment building on the corner of Second Street. There's a restaurant next to the apartment building, and there's a police station next to the restaurant.
A: Oh, I know where that is. OK. See you tomorrow.

Narrator: **Clear your worksheet and listen again.**

A: I'll pick you up. Where do you live?
B: 4433 Washington Avenue. It's a house. It's in the middle of the block, between First and Second streets. There's a big Catholic church on the corner of First, and there's a laundromat right across the street from my house.
A: OK. I'm sure I can find that. See you tomorrow.

Situation B, page 52

Narrator: **These people are describing their neighborhoods.**

A: I love my block. It's really great. I live on Washington Avenue, between First and Second streets. My apartment building is right in the middle of the block. There's a big park next to my house. And next to the park there's a beautiful church, on the corner of Second Street and Washington. Around the corner from the church there's a school. It's an elementary school. My son goes there.

Narrator: **Clear your worksheet and listen again.**

B: I really hate my block. It's terrible. I live in a small house on the corner of Washington Avenue and Second Street. There's a big parking lot across the street from my house, and there are always a lot of cars coming and going. And there's a gas station next to my house, on the left. It's open all night. It's noisy and there's a lot of traffic.

Situation C, page 54

Narrator: **These people are asking about places in the neighborhood.**

A: Excuse me . . . is there a parking lot around here?
B: Uh . . . yeah . . . on the corner of Second Street. Down there.
A: Thanks.
B: Sure.

A: Excuse me, is there a grocery store or a supermarket around here?
B: Yes. See the park, there on the corner of First?
A: Uh-huh.
B: OK. Around the corner from the park, on First Street, there's a big supermarket.
A: On the corner of Washington?
B: No, it's kind of in the middle of the block.
A: Oh, thanks.

Situation D, page 56

Narrator: **This couple needs an apartment. They are visiting a new neighborhood.**

A: This neighborhood is pretty nice. What do you think?
B: I don't know. Does it have what we need?
A: What *do* we need?
B: Well, we need a park. Somewhere to walk the baby.
A: Yeah. Exactly. And there's a park right over there, on the corner of First.
B: We really need a laundromat nearby.
A: I saw a laundromat. There's one around the corner from the restaurant. See the restaurant there, on the corner of Second? Well, there's a laundromat just around the corner on Second Street. And you know what I like? There aren't any liquor stores around here.
B: I don't know . . . The apartment building is on Washington . . . And this Washington Avenue is very busy.
A: Yeah, but it's next to the park. Maybe you can see the park from the apartment.
B: OK. Let's look at the apartment.

CHAPTER 6
At Work, at Home and on Vacation

Situation A, page 62

Narrator: **This is the Acme Computer factory. Some employees are moving boxes from the warehouse.**

A: Excuse me, *(name)* ?
B: Oh, hi *(name)* . How are you doing?
A: Fine. Where do you want the green box?
B: The green one? Uh, put it in the office for now, OK?
A: Sure.

A: Excuse me, *(name)* ?
B: Yes, *(name)* ?
A: You know the red box over there? Where do you want it?
B: The red one? Put it out on the loading dock, would you?
A: OK.

A: *(name)* ?
B: Yeah?
A: Where do you want the blue box?
B: Oh, that's candy for the machine. It goes in the employee lounge.
A: OK.

Situation B, page 64

Narrator: **This is the assembly line of Acme Computers. The boss is looking for some employees.**

A: Oh, *(name)* ?
B: Yes, (Mr./Ms.) *(name)* ?
A: Is Sam at work today?
B: No, he's not here. He's home sick. I think he has the flu.
A: How about Caroline? She's here, isn't she?
B: Yeah. She's down in the warehouse.
A: OK, thanks.

A: Hi, *(name)* .
B: Oh, hi *(name)* .
A: Is Miguel around? I need to talk to him about something.
B: Miguel? I think he's in the employee lounge. It's his break right now.
A: Oh, OK. Thanks.

Situation C, page 66

Narrator: **The boss and an employee are in the office talking.**

A: Hey, *(name)* , we need some help in the warehouse. Where's Joe?
B: He's in the employee lounge taking a break.
A: OK. How about Sam? What's he doing?
B: Sam? I think he's down on the loading dock, loading a truck.
A: Is Caroline here today? She was sick yesterday, wasn't she?
B: Yeah, she's here today. But she's working on the assembly line right now.
A: Who else is on the assembly line?
B: Miguel and Gina, I think.
A: Oh, OK. We can finish the warehouse stuff later.

Situation D, page 68

Narrator: **The boss is calling employees on the intercom.**

A: Is this *(name)* ?
B: Yes, *(name)* .
A: What are you doing right now?
B: I'm still on the assembly line.
A: Is there anyone else there?
B: Yeah. Caroline is here.
A: Good. She can stay there, but I need your help in the office right away.

A: Hi, *(name)* ?
B: Yes, *(name)* ?
A: Are you busy right now?
B: Kind of. I'm in the warehouse helping Kim move some boxes out to the loading dock.
A: OK. After that, could you go up and help out on the assembly line?
B: Sure.

Listen CHAPTER 7

The Supermarket

Situation A, page 74

Narrator: These shoppers are looking for groceries in a busy supermarket.

A: Excuse me, I'm looking for the aspirin.
B: It's in the Pharmacy section. In aisle 1. I think the aspirin is on the bottom shelf toward the front.
A: Thanks.

A: Hi. (*speak softly*) Where's the milk?
B: I'm sorry. The what?
A: The milk.
B: Oh, OK. See the exit sign over there, in the corner?
A: Yes.
B: OK. The milk is next to the exit on the right. In the refrigerator case.
A: OK. Thank you.

Situation B, page 76

Narrator: In a busy supermarket, a clerk helps shoppers find what they need.

A: Excuse me. Do you have a deli section? I can't find the take out food anywhere.
B: Take out food? In the back. It's on the left side of the store.
A: The left side?
B: Yes.
A: Thanks.

A: Excuse me, do you have any mops?
B: Mops? No, I'm sorry, we don't have them. But we do have some brooms in aisle 2.

A: Hi.
B: Hi, can I help you with something?
A: I can't seem to find any lettuce. Where is it?
B: Lettuce? It's on the right side of the store. See that cashier over there? It's right in front of her.
A: Thanks a lot.

Situation C, page 78

Narrator: This couple is at home talking about the groceries they need to buy.

A: Honey, could you go to the store for me?
B: Sure. What do you need?
A: Just pick up some cold cuts. We can have sandwiches.
B: OK. Where are they anyway?
A: The cold cuts are in the back of the store, on the right.
B: OK.
A: Oh, yeah, and could you pick up some coffee too?
B: Coffee? Where's that?
A: When you walk in the store, by the cashier, it's on the left. I think that's aisle 2.
B: In the front of the store, on the left?
A: Yeah.
B: OK. See you in a few minutes.

Situation D, page 80

Narrator: This couple is shopping together in a busy supermarket.

A: How much are the oranges?
B: Let's see . . . uh . . . sixty cents a pound.
A: That's cheap. Let's get some.
B: OK. This lettuce looks pretty nice.
A: How much is it?
B: A dollar twenty-five for one head.
A: That's not cheap. That's expensive.
B: Really?
A: Yeah. Don't get that. Get a different kind.

CHAPTER 8 Your Body

Situation A, page 86

Narrator: This person is at the doctor's office.

A: Hello. I'm Dr. _(name)_.
B: Hi, Doctor. I'm _(name)_.
A: Hi, _(name)_. So, what's up? What's the problem?
B: I don't know Doctor . . . I have this really bad pain in my leg here. It's all down my leg, and in my knee, and even my ankle.
A: How about your foot?
B: No, that's the only place that doesn't have pain.
A: OK. Let's take a look at you.

Situation B, page 88

Narrator: This parent and son are visiting the doctor's office.

A: Good morning, Dr. _(name)_.
B: Well, good morning! Both you and your son are here? Are you both sick?
A: Yes, unfortunately. But we seem to have different things. My son has a fever and a bad cough. I have a bad stomachache.
B: Hmmm . . . I see. And your son doesn't have a stomachache?
A: No.
B: How about you? Do you have a fever? Did you take your temperature?
A: No, I don't have one. I took it this morning. It was 98.6.
B: Well, we'll take both of your temperatures again. Let's have a look at you.

Situation C, page 90

Narrator: This patient is at the doctor's office with a shoulder problem.

A: Good morning. What's up?
B: Hi, Doctor. Well, I get this really bad pain in my shoulder when I play tennis.
A: Hmmm. Well, I looked at your X-rays, and everything seems OK. Do you have any pain in your elbow?
B: No.
A: Any pain anywhere else?
B: No, just my shoulder.
A: OK. Well, I'd like you to try this ointment here. Rub this on your shoulder as soon as you feel any pain. See if that helps you any.
B: OK. Anything else?
A: Well, you can take a couple of aspirin, too. I don't think it's anything serious, or it would show up on the X-rays.
B: OK.
A: Let me know how it goes.
B: OK. Thanks, Doctor.

Situation D, page 92

Narrator: This person is calling the doctor's office to make an appointment.

A: Good morning, Dr. Kwon's office.
B: Yeah, hi. My name is _(name)_. I'd like to make an appointment with the doctor. I have a really bad cough and I think I have a fever.
A: Is tomorrow OK?
B: Is there any chance of getting an appointment today? I really feel terrible.
A: I'm terribly sorry, but the doctor is leaving in a few minutes.
B: OK. I guess tomorrow will have to do.
A: If you feel it's an emergency . . .
B: No, tomorrow will be OK.

CHAPTER 9

The Family

Situation A, page 98

Narrator: On the quiz show "What's the Price?", this person is asked about his/her family.

A: OK, *(name)*, welcome to the show. Tell our audience a little about your family. Are you married?
B: No, I'm still single.
A: Still single, huh? Do you have any plans for the near future?
B: No, not really.
A: OK. How about brothers and sisters?
B: I have one brother, Ron. And I have two sisters, Amy and Mary. They're both here tonight.
A: Both your sisters are in the audience? That's wonderful. Well, wish your (brother/sister) luck, because we're about to play "What's the Price?".

Situation B, page 100

Narrator: This is the next person on the quiz show "What's the Price?".

A: Welcome to the show. Are you married, *(name)*?
B: Yes, I am. My (husband's/wife's) name is *(name)*. (He's/She's) out there in the audience.
A: Well, good for (him/her). Do you have any children?
B: Uh-huh. We have two children. A son and a daughter.
A: That's wonderful. What are their names?
B: My son's name is Alan, and my daughter's name is April.
A: April. That's a nice name. Are they here tonight?
B: Yes, they are. Right down there with my (husband/wife).
A: Well, good luck *(name)*. And let's play "What's the Price?".

Situation C, page 102

Narrator: These friends are showing each other their family pictures.

A: Nice picture, *(name)*. Wow, you really have a big family. Who's that?
B: That's my (wife/husband). (Her/His) name's *(name)*.
A: Are those your kids?
B: Uh-huh. That's my son, Tom and that's my daughter, Kathy.
A: Nice kids. Who's this woman?
B: That's my sister, Susan. And the guy there is her husband, Frank. They've been married for fifteen years.
A: Fifteen years, huh?
B: Yeah, they don't have any kids.

Situation D, page 104

Narrator: Another pair of friends are showing family pictures.

A: Oh, here are some pictures of my family. Would you like to see them?
B: Sure. Let's see.
A: OK. This is my brother.
B: Does he live here?
A: No, he lives in Mexico. And let's see... this is a picture of my (brother/sister).
B: (He's/She's) very attractive.
A: Yes, (he/she) is.
B: Does (he/she) live in Mexico, too?
A: No, (he/she) lives here, just a few blocks away.
B: Maybe I could meet (him/her) sometime.
A: Get out of here! (He's/She's) my (brother/sister)!

Listen **CHAPTER 10**

A Daily Schedule

Situation A, page 110

Narrator: These two friends are talking at work.

A: Hi, _(name)_, how are you doing?
B: OK. I'm kind of tired.
A: Did you get up early today?
B: I get up early every day. At 6 a.m.
A: That's pretty early. What time do you go to bed?
B: I don't usually get to bed until around 1 or so.
A: Really? How come so late?
B: I leave school around ten. Then, when I get home, I have to clean a little before I go to bed.
A: That's a tough schedule.
B: Yeah, but I can do it.

Situation B, page 112

Narrator: These two friends are leaving work together.

A: See you tomorrow morning _(name)_.
B: Yeah, see you _(name)_. Oh geez, I'm late.
A: Late for what?
B: For my class.
A: Oh, you go to school?
B: Yeah. I'm studying computers. My class starts at 5:30.
A: You really have to rush. How long is the class?
B: Class ends at 9:00. It's three and a half hours long.
A: Wow, that's tough to go to work all day and then go to class.
B: Yeah. Well, I gotta go. See you.

Situation C, page 114

Narrator: This news reporter is interviewing a lottery winner.

A: Congratulations on winning the lottery!
B: Thank you.
A: So . . . you won four million dollars. Tell us, how has your life changed? What's different?
B: Well, I don't work anymore. I quit my job.
A: So what do you do everyday?
B: I still get up early—around 7 o'clock. I usually eat breakfast at 8:00 and then watch my favorite program on TV from 10:00 to 11:00. In the afternoon, around 2:00, I like to exercise—I usually lift weights, jog, and swim in my new pool.
A: That sounds like a pretty nice schedule.
B: Yeah, it's okay.

Situation D, page 116

Narrator: This person notices that something is bothering a friend.

A: You look . . . I don't know, unhappy about something.
B: I am. I am bored with my life.
A: What do you mean?
B: Everything is exactly the same every day. First, I shower at 6. After that, I eat breakfast at 6:30. I know it's 6:30 because the same news show is on the TV. At exactly 7:00 I go to work. It's the same every day.
A: Why don't you get up at five tomorrow?
B: Get up at five?
A: Yeah. You can exercise for a while.
B: Hmmm . . . not a bad idea.

School

CHAPTER 1

WORKSHEET

OFFICE
EXIT
FRONT
DOOR
BOOKSTORE
CAFETERIA
Mr. Sanchez
Ms. Williams
MEN
WOMEN
0 1 2 3 4 5 6 7 8 9 0

CHAPTER 2

A Kitchen

WORKSHEET

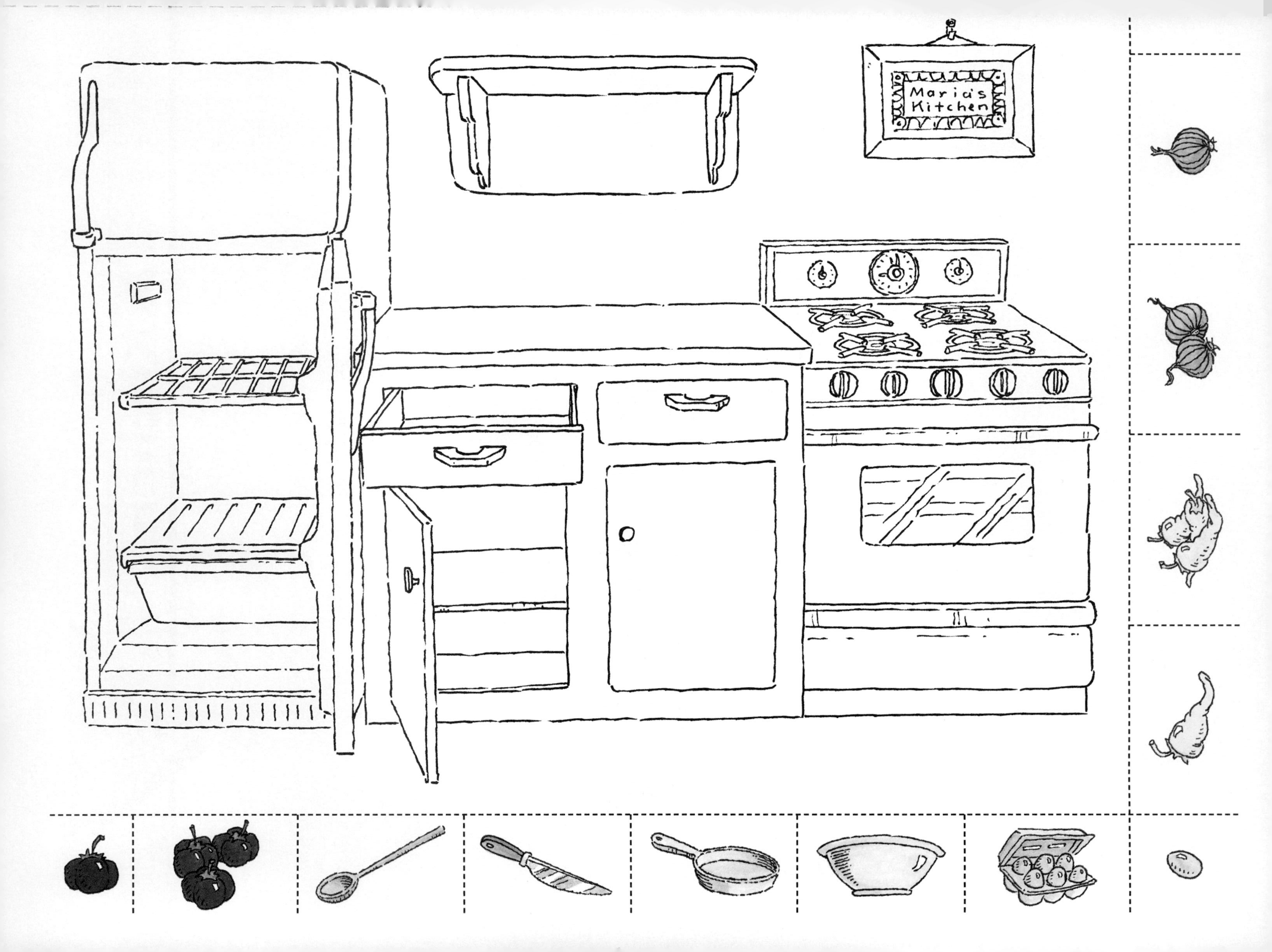

Maria's
Kitchen

CHAPTER 3

Time

WORKSHEET

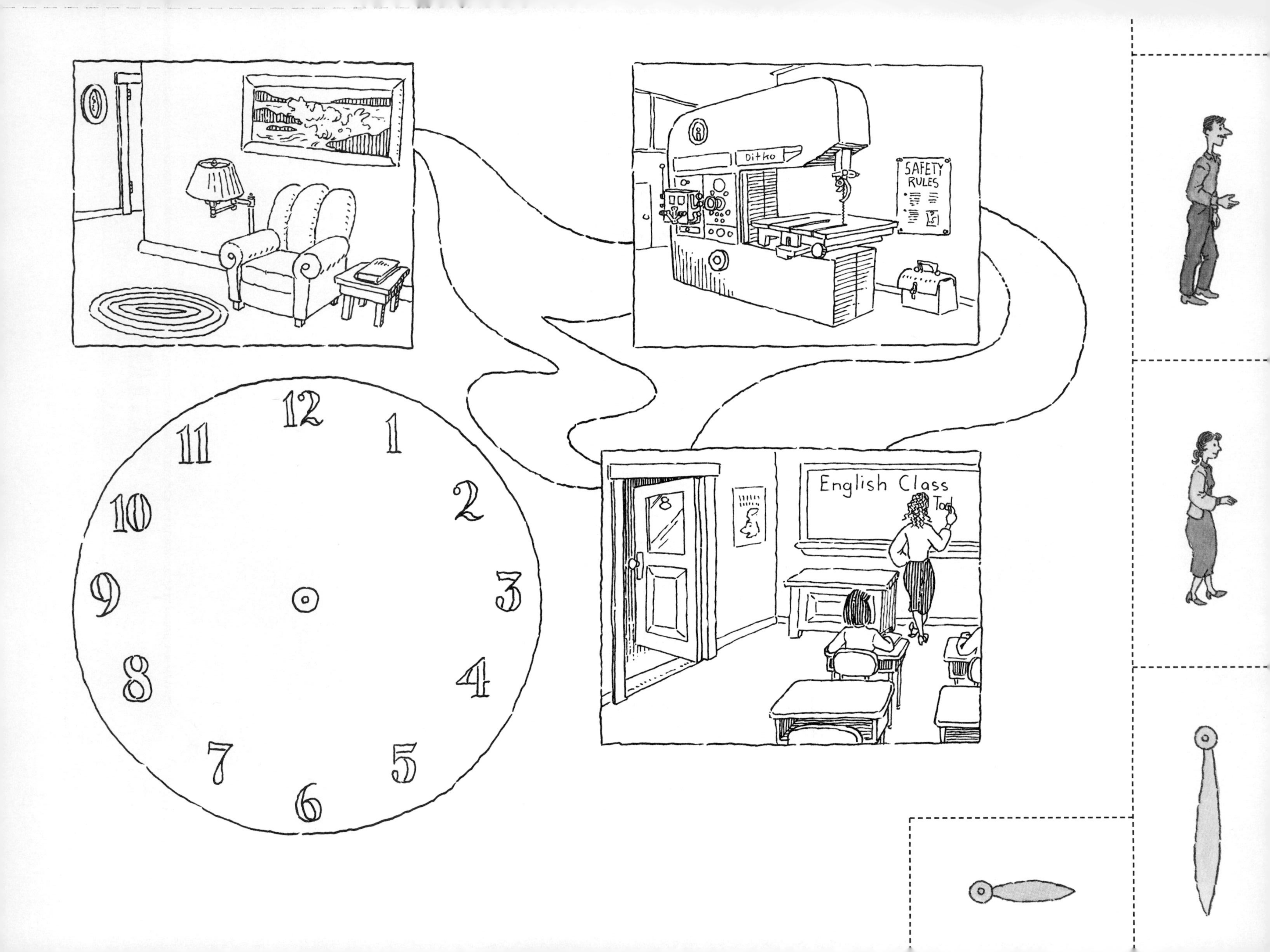

Ditko
SAFETY RULES
English Class
Tod
12
1
2
3
4
5
6
7
8
9
10
11

A Restaurant

WORKSHEET

.45¢
.50¢
.60¢
.75¢
$1.15
$1.25
$1.30
$1.50
$1.80
$1.90

Your Neighborhood

CHAPTER 5

WORKSHEET

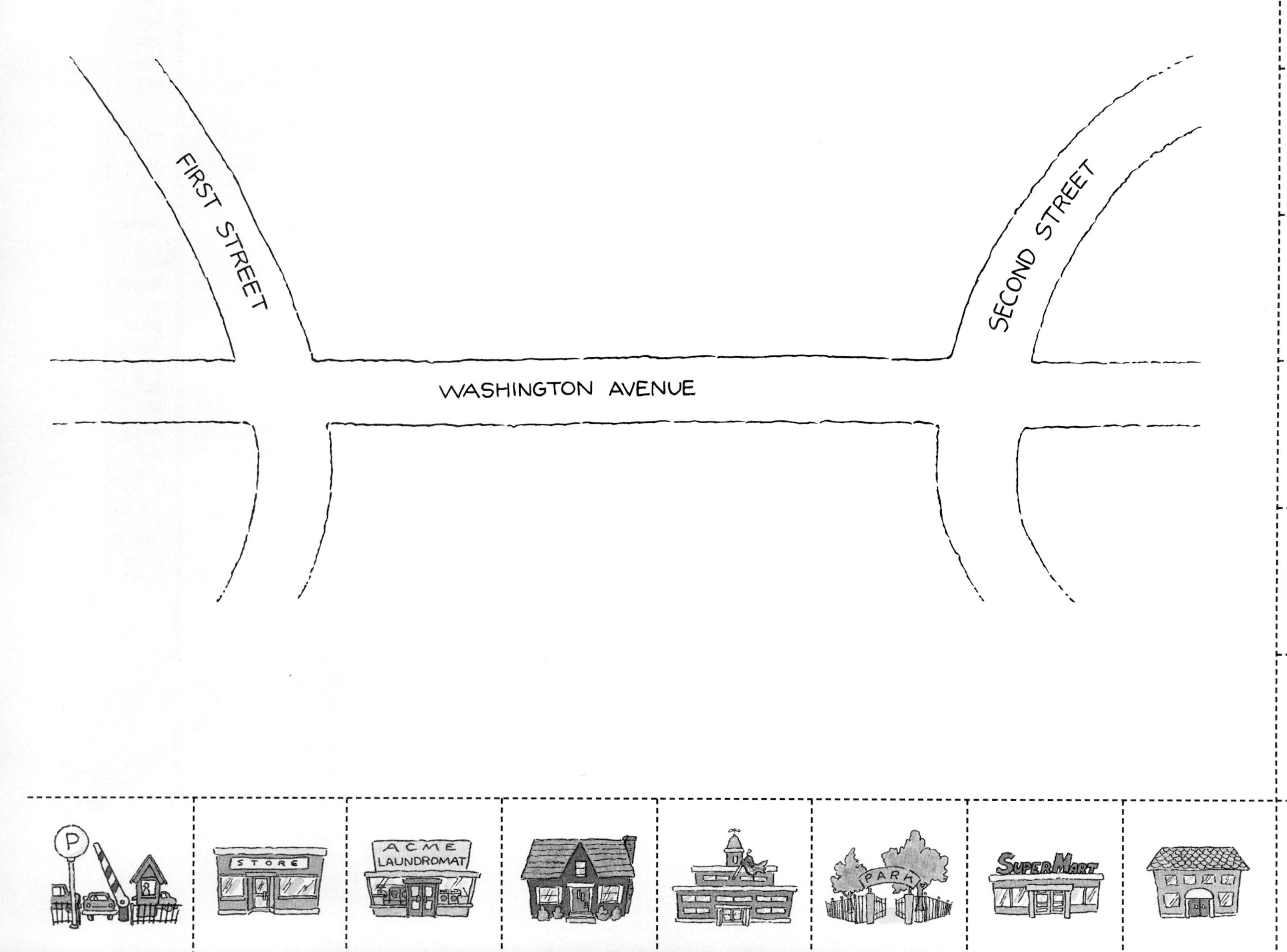
FIRST STREET
SECOND STREET
WASHINGTON AVENUE
STORE
ACME LAUNDROMAT
PARK
SUPERMART
A VACANT LOT

POLICE

GAS
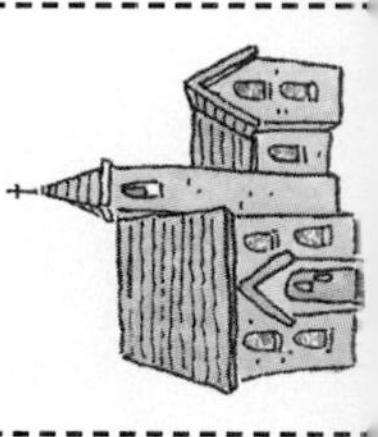

RESTAURANT

OFFICE COMPLEX

At Work, at Home, and on Vacation

WORKSHEET

Caroline

Gina

Joe

Sam

Miguel

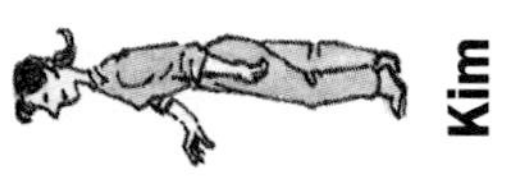
Kim

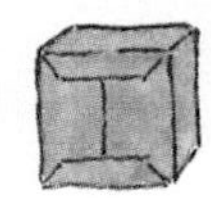

WORKSHEET

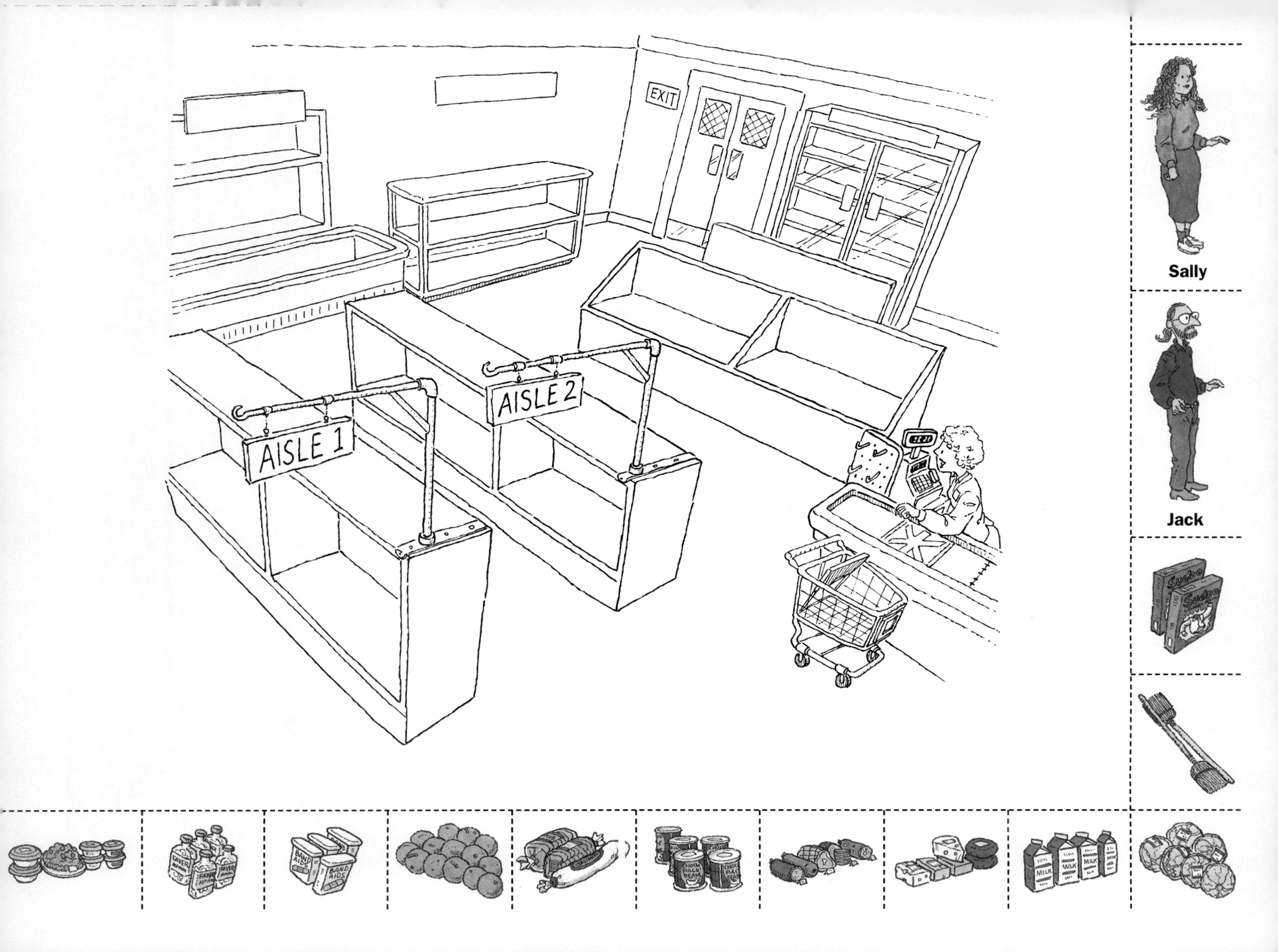
EXIT
AISLE 1
AISLE 2
Sally
Jack
BAND AIDS
MILK

CHAPTER 8

Your Body

WORKSHEET

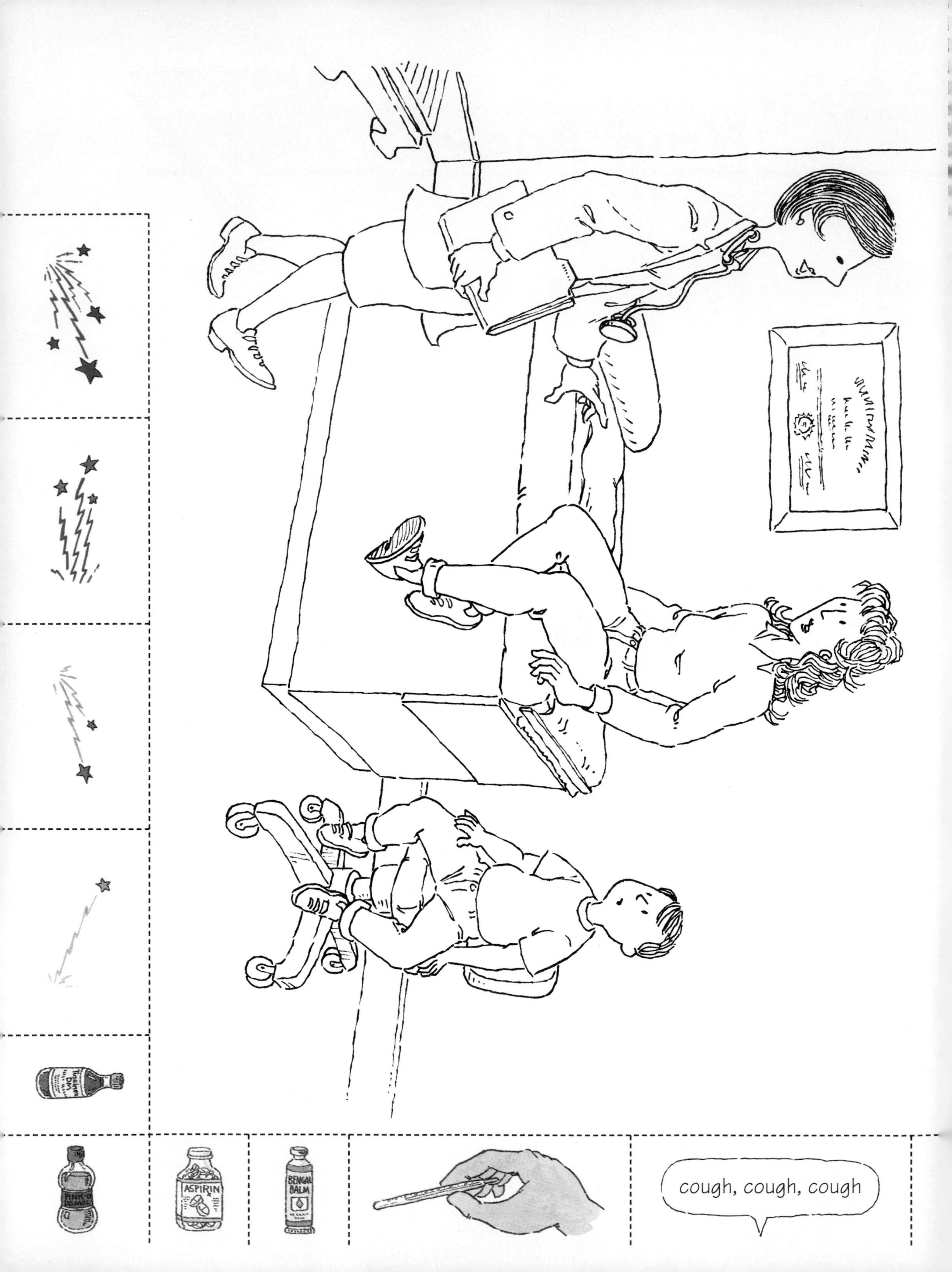
cough, cough, cough
ASPIRIN
BENGAL BALM

The Family

CHAPTER 9

WORKSHEET

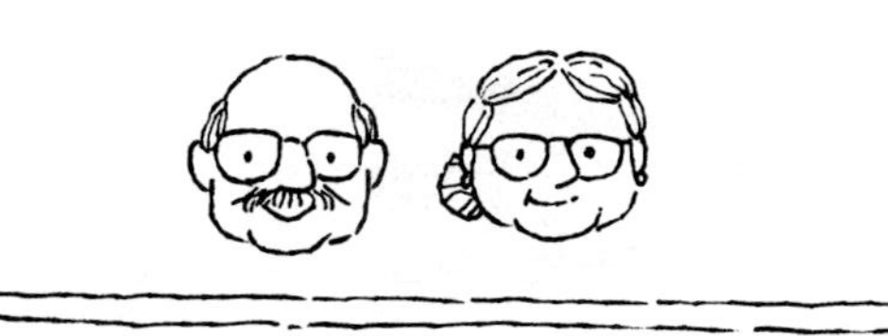

Kathy

Alan

Beth

April

Bob

Frank

Mary

Jim

Ron

Ellen

Amy

Joe

Susan

Tom

WORKSHEET

JFK SCHOOL

JFK SCHOOL

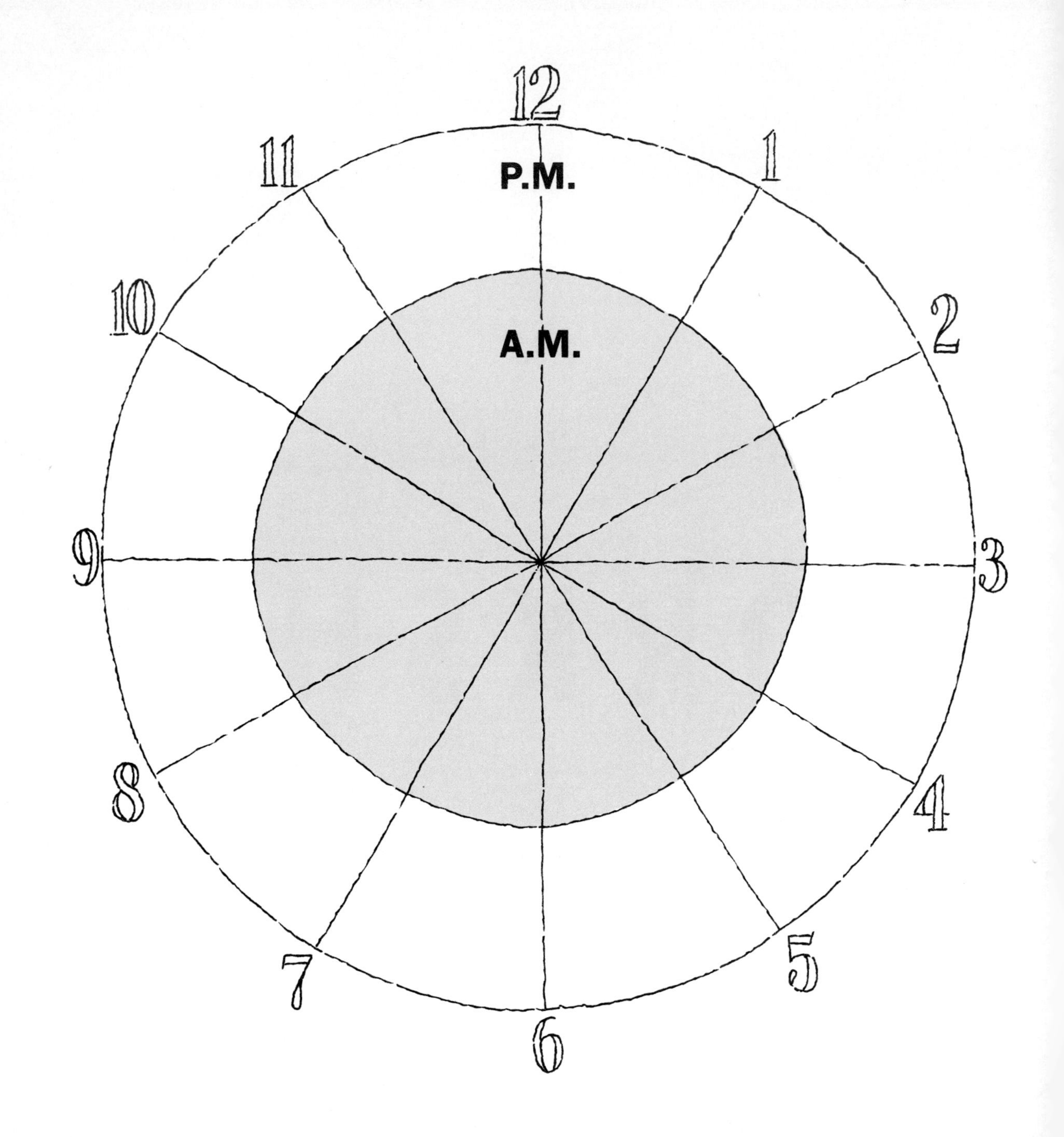
12
1
2
3
4
5
6
7
8
9
10
11
P.M.
A.M.

ACME

ACME